AF886064

To my dear friend Jossi Bamira
dedicated with much affection

by Baruch Berliner

LIMITS OF INSURABILITY OF RISKS

BARUCH BERLINER

Swiss Reinsurance Company
P.O. Box CH-8022 Zurich, Switzerland

Prentice-Hall, Inc., Englewood Cliffs, N.J. 07632

Library of Congress Cataloging in Publication Data

Berliner, Baruch.
Limits of insurability of risks.

1. Risk (Insurance). 2. Insurance.
I. Title. II. Title: Insurability of risks.
HG8054.5.B47 368 81-19909
ISBN 0-13-536789-1 AACR2

Editorial/production supervision and interior design by Richard C. Laveglia
Cover design by Edsel Enterprises
Manufacturing buyer: Ed O'Dougherty

© 1982 by Prentice-Hall, Inc., Englewood Cliffs, N.J. 07632

All rights reserved. No part of this book may be reproduced in any form or by any means without permission in writing from the publisher.

Printed in the United States of America

10 9 8 7 6 5 4 3 2 1

ISBN 0-13-536789-1

Prentice-Hall International, Inc., *London*
Prentice-Hall of Australia Pty. Limited, *Sydney*
Prentice-Hall of Canada, Ltd., *Toronto*
Prentice-Hall of India Private Limited, *New Delhi*
Prentice-Hall of Japan, Inc., *Tokyo*
Prentice-Hall of Southeast Asia Pte. Ltd., *Singapore*
Whitehall Books Limited, *Wellington, New Zealand*

Contents

Foreword

In my opinion Dr. Baruch Berliner, Non-Life Actuary of the Swiss Reinsurance Company, Zurich, has accomplished the difficult task of defining the limits of insurability in his book. He has also managed to turn this extremely important and topical subject affecting many fields of technology into an easily readable and exciting form which does not call for any prior knowledge of mathematics.

The criteria of insurability have been painstakingly analyzed and practical conclusions convincingly drawn. The carefully selected examples are of interest and value.

The book is primarily intended for all those whose job is or will be to determine the cover limits for their company. I believe it will achieve its goal of providing them with useful pointers and decision-making guidelines.

Universities have also been borne in mind. Apart from being practical, the book is also of great theoretical value, as it gives a comprehensive and original survey of the concept of "insurability."

Finally, the book contains surprising elements which will stimulate the intellect of the reader, to whom I wish much pleasure in reading it.

H. B. Vischer
Deputy Chairman of the Board
Swiss Reinsurance Company

Acknowledgments

The impetus to prepare this study came from Mr. H. B. Vischer, Deputy Chairman of the Swiss Reinsurance Company, to whom I should like to express my appreciation.

I also wish to thank Dr. R. Arpagaus, Dr. C. E. Brooks, and Dr. H. K. Zulauf of Swiss Reinsurance Company and Mr. P. J. Turvey, F.I.A., of Swiss Reinsurance Company (UK) Ltd., for giving me the benefit of their expert opinion in the discussion of certain sections of the study.

Finally, valuable support was received from Dr. P. F. Niquille, General Manager, and Mr. J. Roos, Manager of the Swiss

Reinsurance Company, as well as from Dr. Kenneth Black, Dean of the School of Business Administration at Georgia State University.

B. Berliner

Introduction

Advancing technology, social progress, the growth of urban conglomerations and social problems, accumulation problems, possibilities of chain reactions, and the increasing complexity and size of numerous risks are bringing us closer and closer to the limits of insurability, confronting us more and more frequently with the question, "What risks are still insurable?"

A generalized *answer* to this question is *not achievable,* since it will depend upon *subjective considerations.* Nevertheless, an attempt can be made to identify those considerations which are subjective, and to limit them so far as possible in favor of an *objective, generally acceptable viewpoint.*

The practical answers to the question of the insurability of risks will always contain a subjective element, reflecting, for example, the business policy guidelines of an insurance company. Nevertheless, certain *basic objective principles* should be followed.

To examine the question of the *insurability of risks,* it is first necessary to clarify this concept. A general definition, convenient and useful as it might be, *cannot be proposed* because of the subjective content and complexity of the concept, which is why we prefer to subject it to as *clear and comprehensive an analysis as possible.*

In the model which we use for analysis, we will "automatically" *overcome* a complicated and often confusing "interference factor," that is, partial insurability, where an insurer is willing to accept only part of a risk.

We shall set up *criteria* and interpret them as *dimensions of insurability,* which, as with a checklist, have to be gone through individually when assessing a risk in order to obtain a clear answer as to the insurability of the risk.

The analysis of individual criteria will lead us to numerous *basic findings,* which we believe to be convincing and illuminating enough to be accepted as objectively correct. We shall formulate basic findings as *principles* and recommend *measures* and *rules of conduct* as well.

We shall close the study with a discussion of examples of risks at the limits of insurability.

We hope that the following comments will provide a useful aid to answering the increasingly important question, "What risks are still insurable?"

The Criteria of Insurability

The concept "insurability" has a converse, that is, *uninsurability.* As these two concepts mutually exclude each other, there must be a *boundary line or area* between them. The aims of this study will be to mark out the *area of insurability* and to examine the boundary area. We shall set up criteria to mark off this area of insurability as follows:

The Criteria of Insurability

a. Randomness (of the loss occurrence)
b. Maximum possible loss
c. Average loss amount upon occurrence

d. Average period of time between two loss occurrences
e. Insurance premium
f. Moral hazard
g. Public policy
h. Legal restrictions
i. Cover limits

These criteria are not independent of each other. Degree of randomness, moral hazard, and public policy are, for example, criteria which are definitely dependent upon and mutually influence each other. What is important, however, is that none of the nine criteria can be replaced by a combination of the remaining eight. The individual criteria will be considered more closely at a later stage.

Most criteria contain both subjective and objective aspects.

We are going to define now a model upon which we shall base our studies. The model avoids contradictions which can easily be inherent in other model approaches.

Definition 1: We say that a *criterion* is *satisfied,* if it confirms the insurability of a risk.

Definition 2: If at least *one criterion* is *not satisfied* for a certain professional risk carrier, then the respective risk is said to be *subjectively uninsurable* for that carrier.

By *professional risk carriers* we mean insurance companies, pension funds, and other institutions which grant risk covers against payment of a premium. When we speak of risk carriers, it is always professional risk carriers which are meant.

A criterion can be *not* satisfied *independently* or *conditionally.*

Definition 3: A criterion is said *not* to be *satisfied independently* if it can be satisfied *exclusively* by quantitative and/or qualitative changes which directly affect the *criterion itself.*

Definition 4: A criterion is said *not* to be *satisfied conditionally* if it can be satisfied by quantitative and/or qualitative changes which *only* affect *other criteria.*

Example:

If a risk carrier sets an absolute upper limit L on his commitment per event as a matter of business policy, which under no circumstances may be exceeded, then criterion b is not satisfied for him in respect of all those risks which could give rise to a maximum loss larger than L, *independently* of how well the other criteria are satisfied. If, on the other hand, the largest possible loss amounts to 10% of L, the risk carrier will be prepared to grant cover against an appropriate premium; if, however, the premium P offered is regarded as insufficient, he will refuse the risk. *Conditioned* by the inadequate premium offer P, a largest possible loss of $L/10$ can still turn out to be a value which fails to satisfy criterion b.

Conversely, we can reason that the premium P would suffice to cover a risk with a largest possible loss of, say, $L/20$, not however one with a maximum possible loss of $L/10$. *Conditioned* by the level of the largest possible loss of $L/10$ (criterion b), criterion e (insurance premium) turns out not to be satisfied.

This example, together with Definitions 3 and 4, leads to *certain conclusions:*

1. The dependence of the criteria upon each other leads to the possibility that criteria may not be satisfied conditionally.
2. If two criteria are mutually dependent and one of them is not satisfied conditionally in respect of a

certain risk, a certain risk carrier, and the other criterion, then the roles of the two criteria can be exchanged.

3. The statement that a criterion is not satisfied independently is much more rigorous than saying that is is not satisfied conditionally. In the first case the criterion can only be satisfied by changed which affect the criterion itself, but in the second case, also be indirect changes which only relate to other criteria.
4. A criterion is not satisfied if it is not satisfied either independently or conditionally. It is thus, according to Definition 2, perfectly possible for a risk to be subjectively uninsurable although it is not the case for a single criterion that it is not satisfied independently. For subjective uninsurability, it is sufficient that certain criteria be merely not satisfied conditionally.

It is thus not enough when investigating insurability of a risk to go through the criteria of insurability one by one and to check whether each is satisfied without taking into account the influence of some criteria on others.

In the example, criterion b (largest possible loss) was not satisfied independently *only if* the maximum possible loss exceeded the limit L. For a maximum loss equal to $L/10$, however, we could not say that criterion b was not satisfied independently. The same held for the insurance premium criterion e for premium P, for a risk with a maximum possible loss of $L/20$ was in fact insurable against a premium of P. Only the combination $(L/10, P)$ shifted the risk into the area of uninsurability, although it was not necessary for *any* criterion to be not satisfied independently in this connection.

When the risk carrier is faced with the choice of granting cover for a given risk at given terms, or not, he must make a decision. Subjectively, therefore, every risk is either insurable or not for every risk carrier, and one can thus conclude that a risk is *subjectively insurable* if it is *not subjectively uninsurable.*

As we shall soon see, the corresponding statement for objective insurability does not hold. From the objective point of view there are risks which are neither insurable nor uninsurable.

Definition 5: The *subjective area of insurability* consists of the set of all subjectively insurable risks.

Definition 6: The *subjective area of uninsurability* consists of the set of all subjectively uninsurable risks.

The subjective areas of insurability and uninsurability are separated by a dividing line.

Definition 7: We describe the set of all risks for which at least one criterion is not satisfied independently as the *area of absolute uninsurability.*

Definition 8: We call the not absolutely uninsurable part of the uninsurability area the *conditionally uninsurable area.*

This consists of the set of all risks for which every unsatisfied criterion is not satisfied conditionally.

Conclusion:

A risk in the conditionally uninsurable area has *at least two criteria* which are not satisfied conditionally.

Proof*

Let criterion K_1 be conditionally not satisfied because of criterion K_2. Then, by definition, criterion K_1 can be satisfied by quantitative and/or qualitative changes affecting criterion K_2 alone. If the risk could not be rendered insurable by changes not

* The nonmathematically inclined reader may omit this section.

affecting criterion K_2, then the latter would not be satisfied independently and the risk would lie in the area of absolute, not, as assumed, of conditional uninsurability.

It must thus be possible to make the risk insurable by changes which do not affect criterion K_2 and the latter is therefore conditionally not satisfied. If K_2 can be satisfied by changes affecting only criterion K_1, then K_1 and K_2 are called *mutually dependent* criteria. (In the example following Definition 4 the criteria *maximum possible loss* and *insurance premium* are mutually dependent.) With K_1 and K_2, therefore, at least two criteria are conditionally not satisfied, which was to be proved.

We can now easily arrive at the following conclusion: *When investigating the insurability of a risk, the nine criteria of insurability are to be gone through one by one and tested as to whether, taking into account all the previously examined criteria, they are satisfied or not. It is irrelevant in this respect in what order the criteria are gone through.*

If a criterion is not satisfied independently, we will sooner or later in any case become aware of this and of the subjective uninsurability of the risk. If several criteria are not satisfied conditionally, one of them (which one depending on the order of examination) will confirm the subjective uninsurability of the risk. What is important is that this confirmation will definitely emerge during the examination process.

No causal relations between criteria need be taken into account which might influence the order of going through the criteria when examining the insurability of a risk.

By Definition 8 the subjective uninsurability area is the union of the absolute and conditional areas of uninsurability.

We can now extend our considerations to a universe of risk carriers and from the subjective to the objective point of view.

Numerous professional risk carriers restrict their activities for reasons of business policy or statutory regulation to the coverage of risks in certain lines of business and regions. Their views on the insurability of risks lying outside their areas of activity should not be brought into consideration. When we speak of "all professional risk carriers" in the following, we shall refer to those whose opinion on the insurability of a given risk is relevant in this sense.

Definition 9: The *objective area of insurability* is the set of all those risks which are subjectively insurable for *all* professional risk carriers.

Definition 10: A risk is *objectively insurable* if it lies in the objective area of insurability.

Objections can be raised to linking the definition of the objective area of insurability to the totality of all professional risk carriers. If each risk carrier is prepared to cover a certain risk, with a side glance at his competitors, knowing full well that under the given circumstances the risk should not be covered, then, according to our definition, this risk is objectively insurable. The definition is therefore not determined by arguments of reason as to whether a risk *should be* insurable, but by the practical reality of whether it *is* insurable. This definition will, however, not prevent us from subsequently setting up reasonable rules of conduct for risk carriers.

By basing our considerations upon the reaction of professional risk carriers, we can clear many an obstacle encountered when treating the concept of insurability through a definition approach (see, for example, Section 4.5.3).

If even one criterion is not satisfied independently or conditionally, the risk is subjectively (Definition 2) and objectively (Definitions 9 and 10) uninsurable, since there is at least one risk carrier who holds the risk to be subjectively uninsurable.

Definition 11: A risk which is *not* considered *subjectively* insurable by *any* professional risk carrier is *objectively uninsurable.*

Definition 12: The *objective area of uninsurability* comprises *all objectively uninsurable risks.*

Conclusion

All risks for which a certain insurability criterion cannot be considered as satisfied by any risk carrier are objectively uninsurable.

> **Definition 13:** All risks which are objectively neither insurable nor uninsurable are in the *boundary area.* For each risk in the boundary area, there are risk carriers who would consider it as insurable and others as uninsurable. This area is therefore also referred to as the *transition area,* or *gray zone.*

Note: The nine criteria listed do not claim in any way to consititute an exhaustive system for the assessment of the insurability of a risk. Nevertheless, they are the essential criteria which *for most cases* clearly determine the subjective insurability or uninsurability of risks, even though the system of criteria may sometimes appear to be incomplete.

Example of Apparent Incompleteness of the Given System of Criteria

Let us assume a risk for which criterion e (insurance premium) is not satisfied because the premium is too low, and let the assessment of the risk be characterized by great uncertainty. Now it is conceivable that, by thoroughly examining the risk, collecting data about its past experience, and studying similar risks, the uncertainty due to lack of information can be reduced in such a way that the premium formerly considered as being too low is now recognized as acceptable. The risk moves over from the area of uninsurability to that of insurability without anything having been done to the nine insurability criteria. What has changed is something in another criterion not listed, which characterizes the *subjectively recognized uncertainty of risks.*

Why did we call the example an apparent incompleteness of our criteria system? The reason is that the required criterion of subjectively recognized uncertainty of risks is part of the insurance premium criterion, as will be shown in detail in Section 4.4.2. Criterion e can be split up into various elements, which could in turn be listed separately as insurability criteria.

We have sought out the nine comprehensive but still analyzable criteria in such a way that with as few tests as possible a decision can be taken on the insurability of as large a number of risks as possible.

In the example, however, neither the insurance premium nor the other criteria have changed: How is it then possible that the risk which was supposedly *fixed* by the nine criteria could have *crossed over* from the area of uninsurability to that of insurability? With inclusion in the criterion *insurance premium* of the subjectively recognized uncertainty of risks, the *risk could not actually cross over,* but, as a consequence of better information, the professional risk carrier has been able to extend his subjective area of insurability so as to include it. In the example the risk carrier has increased his subjective area of insurability by means of a certain measure (improvement of information).

As a consequence of the analysis of insurability criteria, we shall encounter in Chapter 4 numerous principles, rules of conduct, and recommendations for measures which, as major targets for future achievement, will bring about *either the extension of the subjective insurability area or a modification of certain marginal risks* so that they come to rest in as many subjective areas of insurability as possible.

Of the nine insurability criteria listed, the first five fall essentially in the technical field, the sixth in the field of experience, the seventh under business ethics and the last two are of a legal nature. Criteria e, f, g, and i affect particularly the commercial field.

The Dimensions of Insurability

3.1 GIVING NUMERICAL VALUES TO THE CRITERIA OF INSURABILITY

In contrast to criterion i, cover limits, the remaining eight criteria can be given numerical values. Criteria a to e, degree of randomness, maximum possible loss, average loss amount, average interval between two loss occurrences, and insurance premium, can be arranged quantitatively *according to size.* Criteria f and g, moral hazard and public policy, are less objectively ascertainable than criteria a to e and at first glance it looks as if the assessment will have to be restricted to a *qualitative arrangement* which specifies *subjectively* which of two risks is more subject to moral hazard and which less consistent with public policy.

It can definitely occur that an insurer considers risk *A* to be more subject to moral hazard than risk *B* and that another insurer is of the reverse opinion. If, on the other hand, the largest possible losses of risks *A* and *B* are expressed by the sum insured, then it is no longer in the subjective field of assessment to determine which sum insured is larger.

Moral hazard and public policy thus cannot be treated in a uniform, quantitative manner on the subjective level. We shall, however, show that it is possible to specify a numerical representation to overcome the difficulties just described on the objective level.

In the case of criterion h, legal restrictions, the only question to be answered is whether a cover is legally allowed or not. The two answers will be assigned the values 0 and 1. Consequently, criterion h can also be given a numerical representation.

Why stress the possibility of giving numerical values to the insurability criteria? Because this puts us in a position to represent geometrically the areas of insurability and uninsurability, to illustrate them graphically, and to determine the concept of insurability more precisely.

3.2 THE GEOMETRIC MODEL

Let us now plot the insurability criteria a to h on axes in eight-dimensional Euclidean space and refer to them as *insurability dimensions.* We shall speak of the *a*-axis, *b*-axis, and so on.

On the *a*-axis we do not want to plot the degree of randomness, but 1 minus the degree of randomness so that in the case of *total randomness,* that is, degree 1, the value 0 is assumed and, in the case of risks where occurrence can be predicted *with certainty* at a certain amount and at a certain time, the value 1 is assumed. In between, depending on the degree of randomness, all values between 0 and 1 can be assumed. On the axes *b*, *c*, and *d* all values between 0 and infinity can be assumed (so as to include the unlimited liability covers usual in many countries). If the insurance premium is expressed in monetary units, it can also assume all values between 0 and infinity on the *e*-axis. On the *e*-axis we shall not plot the insurance premium but its reciprocal, so that with a nil premium the value on the *e*-axis is infinite and, as the insurance premium increases, the value on the *e*-axis moves toward 0.

In the objective sense, the criteria *moral hazard* and *public policy* should be allowed to assume certain values between 0 and 1 on the *f*- and *g*-axes, where the value 0 is assumed in the case of generally recognized absence of moral hazard (by all risk carriers) or absolute consistency with public policy, and the value 1 for the converse cases. On the *h*-axis the criterion of legal restrictions should only be able to assume the values 0 and 1, in other words, the value 0 when the risk can be covered within the legal restrictions by *one* policy, the value 1 when it *cannot* be covered by *any* policy.

Figure 1

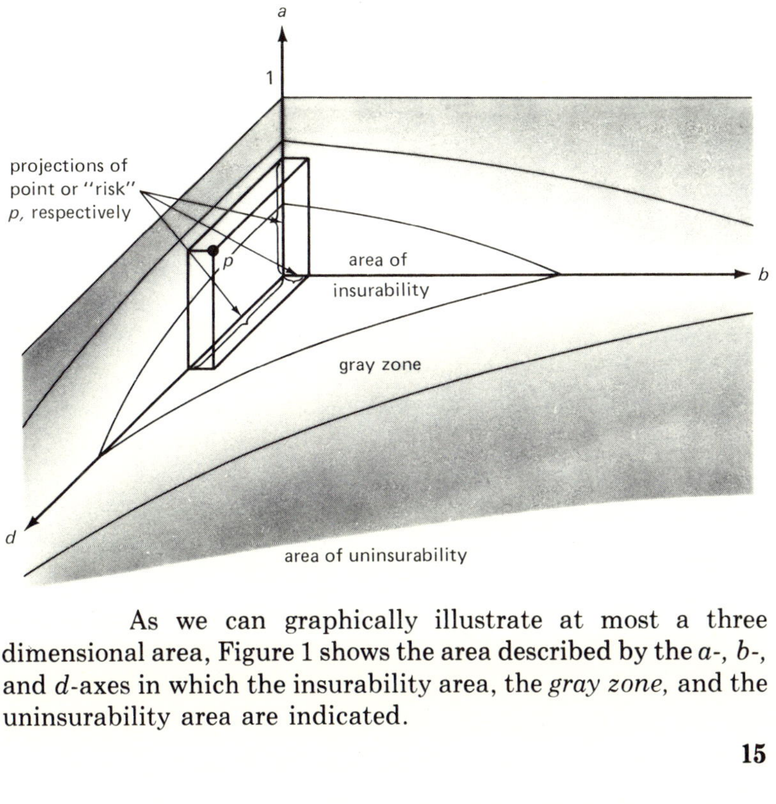

As we can graphically illustrate at most a three dimensional area, Figure 1 shows the area described by the *a*-, *b*-, and *d*-axes in which the insurability area, the *gray zone,* and the uninsurability area are indicated.

We have chosen the numerical representation of the criteria on all eight axes in such a way that the area of insurability should be concentrated around the origin (for the sake of simplicity, we have ignored the possibility of negative values, as might, for example, be conceivable on the a-axis). The area of insurability is surrounded by the gray zone, which is in turn surrounded by the area of uninsurability.

A point near the origin represents a risk for which:

1. Losses occur with a high degree of randomness.
2. The maximum possible loss is very limited.
3. The average loss amount upon loss occurrence is small.
4. The average time interval between two loss occurrences is small (i.e., losses occur frequently).
5. The insurance premium is very high.
6. There is hardly any possibility of moral hazard.
7. Coverage of the risk is consistent with public policy.
8. The law permits the cover.

From an insurance point of view, such risks are ideal and belong in the area of insurability.

Each risk corresponds to one point in the eight-dimensional space, which can be located in the insurability area, in the gray zone, or in the uninsurability area. However, several risks can be allocated to one point.

The area of insurability can be imagined as a white zone which blends into a light gray zone along the boundary line to the boundary area. The boundary area becomes generally increasingly darker the farther away we move from the origin. Finally, the dark gray area blends into the black area of uninsurability.

The shade of the gray zone suggests the *degree of insurability* of the risks. In the light gray zone we find risks which are regarded by the majority of risk carriers as insurable and only by a minority as uninsurable. The farther we move into the gray area (i.e., the darker the boundary area becomes), the greater becomes the number of risk carriers considering the risks as uninsurable and the more the degree of insurability of the risks decreases.

We can construct the gray zone as follows: In the lightest gray area, we take all those risks which are considered to be uninsurable by only one single professional risk carrier. We shall not go into the still finer distinction here which would indicate how the risk might be brought from the lightest gray area into the objective area of insurability: whether the one risk carrier rejecting the risk rejects it because of one or several criteria, whether these are not satisfied conditionally or independently, and so on. The next shaded zone comprises risks which are recognized by two risk carriers as being uninsurable. We continue in this way until we reach the periphery of the gray zone containing risks only regarded as insurable by a single risk carrier.

If we now apply the same procedure to the insurability criteria f and g (i.e., moral hazard and public policy), then it is also possible to determine in the objective sense a representation for these criteria as follows: Let the number of all risk carriers be N. All risks which would not be rejected by a single risk carrier because of moral hazard are given the value 0 on the f-axis. All risks refused by a single risk carrier because of moral hazard are plotted on the f-axis with the value $1/N$. Finally, all risks which only a single risk carrier would *not* reject because of moral hazard are plotted with the value $(N\text{-}1)/N$ and the risks which would be rejected by all risk carriers with the value $N/N=1$.

We proceed in the same way in quantifying the evaluation on the basis of public policy on the g-axis, thereby achieving a quantification of all the criteria of insurability a to h from the objective—not subjective—point of view.

Remark on the Subjective Area of Insurability

In Section 3.1 we saw that the criteria *moral hazard* and *public policy* cannot be uniformly, quantitatively represented at the subjective level. Also, for other criteria it is not subjectively necessary for every risk carrier to assign the same value to a particular risk. Let us imagine two equally large risk carriers *A* and *B* with similar portfolios who wish to determine the degree of randomness of a given risk *R*. Suppose that the risks in risk carrier *A*'s portfolio are independent of *R*, whereas a danger of cumulation exists with those in risk carrier *B*'s portfolio. Risk carrier *A* would likely assign a higher degree of randomness to the risk *R* than would risk carrier *B*, who recognizes that *R* depends to some extent on other risks in his portfolio. But if we assign two different points in the insurability areas of *A* and *B* to the same risk, then although a subjective geometric model for each risk carrier is still possible, a general, objective geometric model such as we have described in this section is no longer possible.

We must therefore *first* define a *unique, objective* risk-point mapping in eight-dimensional Euclidean space for all risks, which satisfies all the required characteristics, and then determine the subjective areas of insurability consisting of all the subjectively insurable "points" in this space. The objective mapping can of course lead to rather bizarre forms of subjective insurability areas in the objective mapping space.

The previously described risk carriers *A* and *B* would then assign the same degree of randomness, dependent upon *all* risks and not merely those in a specific portfolio, to the risk *R* in the objective mapping space. Essential for us in the objective mapping space is the uniqueness of the assignment risk → point as well as the fact that the gray zone covers the objective insurability area and that the subjective areas of insurability are so formed that it is evident for each risk whether its assigned point lies in the subjective insurability or uninsurability area. The last requirement may not be satisfied in exceptional cases. If, specifically, one point corresponds to several risks, of which some are insurable for an individual risk carrier and the others are not, then this point lies on the boundary line between the subjective insurability and uninsurability areas in the objective mapping space. We must accept this disadvantage with an objective geometric model of insurability area, gray zone, and uninsurability area. In a subjective mapping space it is of course not necessary that the boundary line between insurability and uninsurability areas contain a point corresponding to different risks.

We can now state the following: The objective area of insurability is the largest area contained in all subjective insurability areas in the objective mapping space. The objective uninsurability area is the largest area outside all subjective areas of insurability in the objective mapping space. Between the objective areas of insurability and uninsurability lies the gray zone, the construction of which was described earlier in this section.

3.3 THE IMPORTANCE OF THE GEOMETRIC MODEL

By mapping risks as points in eight-dimensional space, we have succeeded in quantifying the various criteria and thus grasping them better. Clear definitions of the insurability, boundary, and uninsurability areas were given in Chapter 2.

We have been able to determine an *objective allocation,* and it does not bother us that, for example, one insurer considers risk *A* to be uninsurable because it is more subject to moral hazard than risk *B*, which he considers to be insurable, whereas another insurer is of exactly the reverse opinion. This fact merely proves that risk *A* is in the uninsurability area of one insurer and risk *B* in that of the other. The two areas overlap. Both risks, *A* and *B*, are in the gray zone. If more risk carriers were to refuse to cover risk *B* than risk *A* because of moral hazard, the projection of risk *A* of the *f*-axis would assume a smaller value than that of risk *B*.

With the gray zone gradually darkening outward toward the area of uninsurability, we have grasped the critical, controversial area optically. Many may find it easier to grasp the concept of insurability in the graphic form of a geometric model rather than in the usual abstract form. The geometric model illustrates why it is impossible to give a general definition of the insurability of risks: It is because of the existence of the gray zone.

Let us now show by means of examples how the abstract notion of insurability can be more clearly understood with the help of the geometric model.

Example 1:

Assume that risk carrier A is only prepared to insure risks up to a maximum possible loss L (criterion b) and that the average time interval between two claim events (criterion d) must not exceed T. Risk carrier A adheres strictly to the limit L irrespective of the claim frequency and to the limit T regardless of the maximum possible loss. His subjective area of insurability in respect of criteria b and d then has the appearance in the geometric model in Figure 2. The rectangular area of insurability

Figure 2

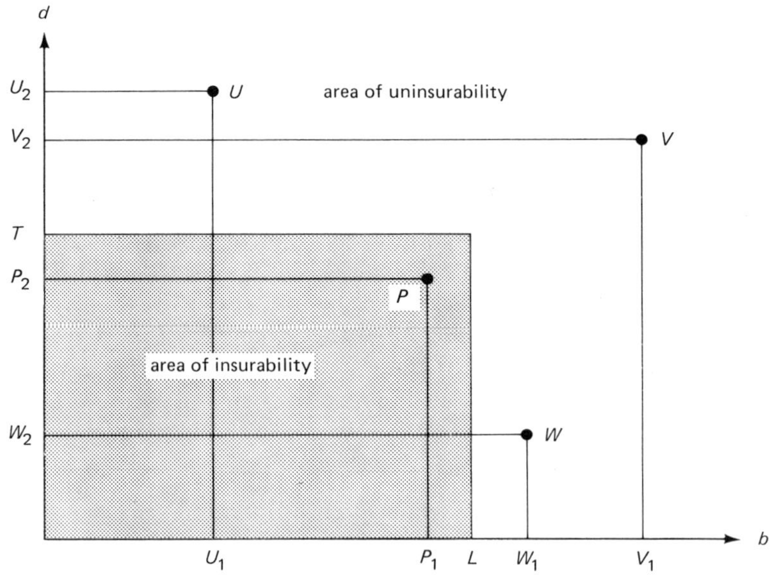

characterizes the (subjective) independence of criteria b and d. For every point P within the area of insurability, the *projections* P_1 and P_2 on the b and d axes are smaller than L and T respectively (i.e., they lie likewise within the area of insurability).

As Figure 2 shows for the points *U*, *V*, and *W* in the area of uninsurability, either one projection is greater than *L* (W_1) or greater than *T* (U_2), or both projections are greater than *L* and *T* (V_1, V_2): at least one projection therefore lies in the area of uninsurability.

The projections which lie in the area of uninsurability correspond to the statement that the corresponding criterion (b or d) is not satisfied independently. Since risk carrier *A* regards criteria b and d as independent of each other, it is impossible for either criterion to be not satisfied conditionally for any risk within the context of these two dimensions only.

Example 2:

Let us again consider criteria b and d, for which a risk carrier *B* once again only permits maximum values of *L* and *T*, respectively. Risk carrier *B*, however, holds these two criteria to

Figure 3

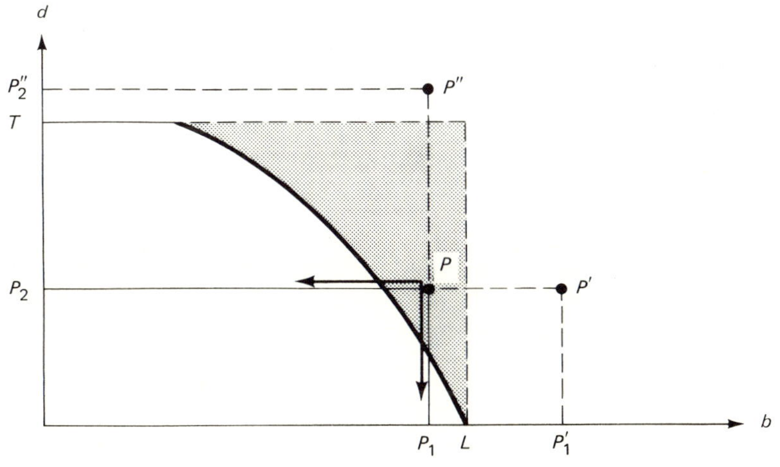

be dependent on each other. If he allows the limit for the maximum possible loss to *rise* with increasing claim frequency (i.e., decreasing average time interval between two claim events), his area of insurability will correspond to Figure 3; if he *reduces* this limit as the claim frequency increases, his area of insurability will assume the form shown in Figure 4.

Figure 4

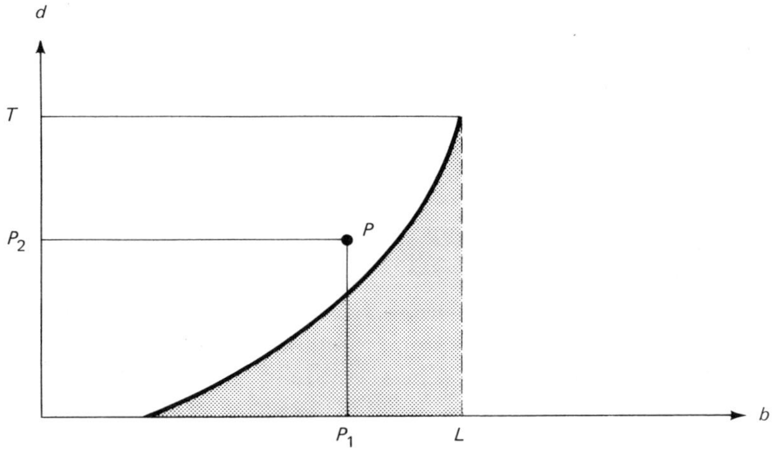

When criteria are dependent on each other, areas of insurability no longer have rectangular form in the geometric model. Changes in the dependence relations result in changes in the form of the area of insurability. Conversely, the type of dependence relations can be deduced from the geometric form of the area of insurability.

As compared with Figure 2, the shaded areas in Figures 3 and 4 have been added to the area of uninsurability as a result of criteria which are not satisfied conditionally. The arrows in Figure 3 suggest how both criteria b and d can be satisfied by a change in only one of them.

If the limits L and T are the same for both risk carriers A and B, we see that B's area of insurability shrinks as compared with A's by exactly the area of conditional uninsurability.

In Example 2 (Figures 3 and 4) the area of absolute uninsurability consists of the domain outside the smallest rectangle drawn on the axes containing the area of insurability. As soon as a point or risk lies outside this rectangle (e.g., points P' and P'' in Figure 3), then at least one of the two criteria is not satisfied independently. The area of conditional uninsurability consists of the portion of the uninsurability area lying within this rectangle (shaded surface). In the case of n criteria (n greater than 2), the rectangle is replaced by a corresponding n-dimensional polyhedron and the reasoning carried through as before.

The geometric model allows us now to determine for which risk carriers an area of conditional uninsurability exists, how large and of what form it is, and to extend our considerations to groups of risk carriers in specific lines of business and geographic areas (i.e., from the subjective to the objective level) in a precise way. We shall not pursue these theoretical aspects, as important as their practical consequences may be, since this would take us beyond the scope of the present study.

Let us return to Example 2. In Figure 3 we have indicated a point P in the area of conditional uninsurability, both projections of which, P_1 and P_2 , lie in the area of insurability. In Figure 4, on the other hand, we were able to draw in a point P in the area of insurability having a projection P_1 on the b-axis lying in the area of conditional uninsurability. *Projections of points within the rectangle which characterizes the area of absolute uninsurability must* therefore *not be used as criteria for the insurability or uninsurability of a risk (point).* Only when a projection is larger than an independent limit (as in Example 1) can we say that the risk in question lies in the area of uninsurability—indeed in the area of *absolute* uninsurability.

Example 3:

Let us imagine a risk carrier C who is prepared to cover any risk regardless of size (criterion b) as long as the premium for his commitment (criterion e) is set accordingly. In the extreme case, of course, he can demand a premium larger than his commitment so that he no longer runs any risk. Whether other criteria, such as legal restrictions, are satisfied does not interest us for the moment, since we wish to concentrate on the criteria b and e.

Figure 5 illustrates the behavior of risk carrier *C*, where the *reciprocal* of the premium is measured on the *e*-axis. The projections of any point whatever lie in the area of insurability. The absolute limits for the maximum possible loss and for the reciprocal of the minimum premium are in principle infinite. The smallest rectangle containing the area of insurability laid on the axes is infinitely large. The entire area of uninsurability consists of the conditionally uninsurable area.

Figure 5

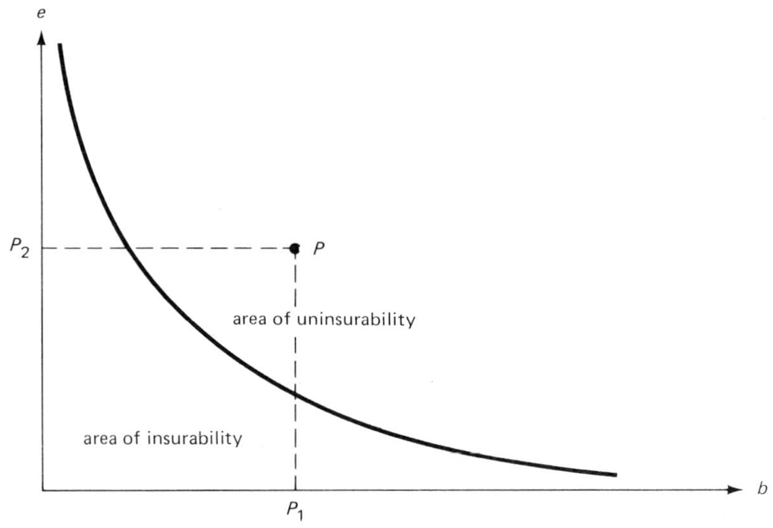

This example is intended to show how the theory behaves in extreme cases and how easily the latter can be illustrated by means of the geometric model. (In reality, of course, there are no claims of arbitrarily large size; on the other hand, free coverage within bouquet covers may exist.)

The quantification and illustration achieved through use of the geometric model permit us to decide what measures must be taken in respect of what criteria to render a given risk insurable, how rigorous these measures must be, and, in the case of criteria which are not satisfied conditionally, what possible alternative measures are available.

3.4 SOME REMARKS

A

Now that we have clearly distinguished between the conditional and the absolute parts of the area of uninsurability, we shall restrict ourselves to essentials in the analysis of the individual criteria in Chapter 4 and, in particular, only occasionally, when it seems especially important, deal with the influence of criteria on other criteria. We are interested primarily in whether and why risks lie on the limits of insurability, and what principles, measures, and rules of conduct are relevant to such critical risks.

We shall no longer distinguish between criteria which are subjectively not satisfied conditionally and those not satisfied independently, and shall leave it to the reader to carry the analysis of insurability farther than is done in this study.

The existence of criteria which are not satisfied conditionally led us first to define subjective *uninsurability* and only then subjective *insurability* as the complement thereof. In accordance with conclusion 4 of Chapter 2, it would be erroneous to attempt a direct definition analogous to that of subjective uninsurability, that is, to state that a risk is subjectively insurable if all criteria are satisfied for a given risk carrier.

B

Dimensions a to h only form a *conditionally complete system*. We had to disregard criterion i (cover limits) in the geometric model as it could not be given a numerical representation. Therefore, an uninsurable risk, one which is not sufficiently protected by cover limits and thus fails to satisfy criterion i, can still be assigned a point in the eight-dimensional insurability area. We should first check whether criterion i is met, and only if it is, then proceed to the geometric mapping of the risk.

In remark 3 in Section 4.4.1 a certain incompleteness of the system of criteria a to i will be revealed. This is, however, of little practical importance and can therefore be disregarded when determining the limits of insurability of risks.

The areas of insurability and uninsurability and the boundary area do not fill up the eight-dimensional Euclidean space. Not every point in the eight-dimensional space represents at least one risk. Thus, for example, a point having a projection on the c-axis larger than that on the b-axis does not represent a risk, since the average loss amount cannot be larger than the maximum possible loss for any risk.

C

The subjective boundary lines of any risk carrier will change with time. In our example at the end of Chapter 2, a risk became insurable as better information led to reduced subjective insecurity. However, it takes time to collect and evaluate information. The subjective area of insurability increased with time in our example, and certain risks previously regarded as uninsurable were included. It was not the mapping risk → point which changed, but the subjective area of insurability itself.

By means of this example, we can deduce that the limits of the objective and subjective insurability and uninsurability areas can change with time, as can the shades of the gray zone. They flow with time.

D

When defining the objective insurability and uninsurability areas, we spoke with a certain reservation of "all professional risk carriers." In fact, however, we know neither all professional risk carriers nor their views on insurability.

If, on the other hand, we are interested in the objective insurability of risks in a certain line of insurance business in a certain region, and if we know the views of a representative number of professional risk carriers in this region and line of business, then we can define and examine "objective insurability" under these given conditions in the same way as before. Nevertheless, we suspect how difficult it is, and under what restricting conditions, to determine an objective insurability area, which moreover changes gradually with time in a real-life situation.

However, we also surmise that each professional risk carrier is mainly interested in his own subjective insurability area and that he only looks at the objective insurability (and even more the boundary) area for competitive reasons.

E

Let us assume a major risk which cannot be covered by a single risk carrier but which can be covered in its entirety by the market as a whole (i.e., by all risk carriers together). As the risk as a totality would be declined by each individual risk carrier, it would fall in the uninsurability area. This result is unsatisfactory, since the risk can still be covered in full by the whole market. We can escape from this dilemma by including in the set of all professional risk carriers not only all insurance companies, pension funds, and the like, but all possible combinations of risk carriers (e.g., pools, insurer and reinsurer). In so doing we can leave all our former definitions and considerations unchanged.

F

The objective area of insurability would normally include numerous "classical" risks in the large lines of business such as life or group life policies, motor third-party liability, or household insurances.

G

According to remark D we can define objective insurability in a given line of business. In the areas specific to this line of business, all the considerations made previously can be repeated.

Let us now examine a risk which, from a technical point of view, has to be split up among several lines of insurance and where values assumed by criteria such as insurance premium have to be split up accordingly. Let us assume moreover that, when considered in the light of certain specific lines of business, parts of the risk are subjectively insurable, whereas others are subjectively uninsurable. Then the risk is in toto subjectively uninsurable. A compound risk is only subjectively insurable if it can be subdivided into a number of basic risks, all of which are insurable according to *all* specific lines of business considerations (i.e., when for each line of business the risk lies in the insurability area of that line of business). A risk carrier is assumed here who is prepared in principle to issue covers in all the lines of business among which the risk must be apportioned.

Example

Let us consider a combined engineering and fire risk, the engineering risk being underrated but the fire risk being overrated in such a way that the risk in toto is not underrated. The risk carrier can obtain the attractive fire risk only on the condition that he also covers the underrated engineering risk. Then the total premium can and should be split up by the risk carrier for *internal* purposes in such a way that neither the fire nor the engineering risk is underrated. A part of the fire risk premium is thus assigned to the engineering risk premium, since only the latter risk enables the risk carrier to obtain the attractive fire risk, and this possibility is worth some "premium amount."

It is this split-up that we refer to in remark G, following our principle that the decision as to whether a risk—in toto or in a single line of business—is insurable or not hinges upon the risk carrier's assessment.

Analysis of the Criteria of Insurability

4.1 DEGREE OF RANDOMNESS

4.1.1 *Degree of Randomness and Correlation Coefficient*

In the geometric model the quantity (1 minus the degree of randomness) was allowed to pass through all values between 0 and 1 on the a-axis, the value 0 having been allocated to *total randomness* and the value 1 to *absolute predictability* of events. This method of representation is based on the possibility of describing the degree of randomness, at least partially, by the precisely defined concept of the *correlation coefficient,* the application of which can be very useful in practice. The *empirical correlation coefficient* can be calculated directly from measurements of at least two sets of data. The correlation coefficient can assume all values between −1 and +1.

If one loss event can be the cause of another, there exists a positive correlation. There would be a negative correlation if, with some positive probability, a loss could entail a gain or reduce the likelihood of a further loss in future. Since mainly positive correlations are of interest for this study, negative correlations will be dealt with only in remarks 2 to 5 of this section and otherwise be ignored. Therefore, when we refer below simply to "correlations," we shall mean "positive correlations."

How does the positive correlation coefficient describe the degree of randomness? If the degree of randomness is equal to 1, the correlation coefficient must always be 0. On the other hand, there are cases where the correlation coefficient is equal to 0 and the degree of randomness is smaller than 1. This can also be expressed as follows: For the degree of randomness to be 1, it is necessary but not sufficient that the correlation coefficient be equal to 0.

In the case of total dependence of one risk on another (degree of randomness equal to 0), the reverse applies. A correlation coefficient that is equal to 1 always signifies total dependence. Total dependence, however, does not necessarily imply that the correlation coefficient must be equal to 1; it can also be smaller. For the degree of randomness to be 0, it is sufficient but not necessary that the correlation coefficient be equal to 1.

The correlation coefficient enables us to calculate the degree of randomness on the basis of statistics and to check the reliability of the results.

Remark 1

A correlation exists *between* risks, describing the dependence of one risk on others. If the occurrence of a certain claim event which is independent of any other claim events can be predicted with some certainty (e.g., an earthquake), the correlation coefficient is often not suitable for describing this fact (see the following sections).

Remark 2

Portfolios from various lines of business may be negatively correlated with each other (e.g., war may result in *increased* mortality ratios but at the same time lead to *reduced* car accident frequency because of less traffic). Negative correlations may sometimes also be found between loss frequency and the average loss amount.

Remark 3

Negative correlations in the portfolio of a risk carrier have a stabilizing effect on the overall result, because a claim (negative result) in a given line of business has a positive effect in reducing the probability of further claims (negative results) in that line or on the results of other lines of business (see Remark 2).

Remark 4

A reinsurance cover should not be so designed as to allow the results of risk carriers and their reinsurers to be negatively correlated. Otherwise, each contractual party would be interested in doing harm to the other. Quota-share reinsurance means, if we disregard commissions, absolute sharing of the fortunes; there is a correlation coefficient equal to +1 between the results of the insurer and those of the reinsurer. Surplus and nonproportional reinsurance represent a *partial* sharing of the fortunes (i.e., there is a positive correlation with a correlation coefficient of *less* than 1).

Remark 5

It would be perfectly possible to consider negative correlations in our geometric model; however, this would lead to complications beyond the framework of this study.

4.1.2 *Two Meanings of the Degree of Randomness*

The degree of randomness of events can be found in two forms, (1) as a complementary concept to the *degree of predictability as a result of noninsurance factors* (such as economic depression), and (2) as a complementary concept to the *degree of dependence on other random events.* The correlation coefficient is generally suited to describing the degree of dependence, but less so to expressing the degree of predictability as a result of noninsurance factors.

As a complementary concept to the degree of dependence on other random events, the degree of randomness of an event is only important for the risk carrier insofar as the latter's portfolio also includes, in addition to a specific risk, other risks on which this specific risk depends. A loss event affecting other risks in the portfolio may also affect the specific risk. This is referred to as the risk of *accumulation.*

Principle 1

> The greater the probability of other risks in the portfolio being affected when a risk is hit by a loss event, that is, the higher the risk of contagion or of accumulation, the lower the degree of randomness from a subjective point of view.

Under certain circumstances a risk carrier can, by laying off particular risks, transform his subjective area of insurability in such a way that a risk dependent upon the risks laid off, which was originally located in the subjective uninsurability area, comes to lie in the insurability area.

If a risk is independent of all other risks in the

portfolio, the risk carrier can determine the degree of randomness of the risk merely by taking account of the degree of predictability of occurrence of a loss event as a result of noninsurance factors within a particular time interval.

Principle 2

> **Total randomness only arises when both the degree of predictability as a result of noninsurance factors and the degree of dependence on other random events are equal to zero.**

It would have been easier to work with a dependence axis than with the randomness axis and to enter on the a-axis the degree of dependence of one risk on others instead of (1 minus the degree of randomness). However, as we have seen, the degree of dependence is only one of two possible complementary concepts of the degree of randomness. We would not have been able to cover the concept of the degree of randomness completely by means of the concept of the degree of dependence on other random events alone.

4.1.3 *Degree of Randomness and the Law of Large Numbers*

In the following paragraph the degree of randomness will be exclusively used as a complementary concept to the degree of dependence on other random events. The law of large numbers implies that estimates of future events are all the more reliable, the larger the number of losses, the more extensive the loss statistics available. As a result, the *loss fluctuations* in a portfolio affected by, say, 10,000 losses will be much *smaller in relation to the total loss* than the relative fluctuations in a portfolio of similar risks which is affected by some 100 losses only.

Note: The expected *absolute fluctuations* of the total loss results *rise* as the portfolio expands; however, the increase is less than the related increase in premium volume and expected total loss. The relative loss fluctuations therefore decline as the portfolio expands.

Example 1

If a large portfolio covers 100 times more risks than a smaller one, and all risks are similar and *independent* of each other (degree of randomness 1), then the expected *relative fluctuations* of the total loss in the larger portfolio will be 10 times less than those in the smaller portfolio. (The expected *absolute* fluctuations will be 10 times higher in the larger portfolio.) We can also say that a *spread* which is 10 times better is achieved in the larger portfolio. *The spread of risks in a portfolio is thus measured by the relative and not by the absolute fluctuations of the total loss result.* There is usually a danger of accumulation among the various risks which, as is to be expected, increases as the number of risks covered rises. Thus the larger risk carrier will achieve a spread which is actually less than 10 times better than that of the smaller carrier. Generally, it can be said:

Principle 3

> The higher the degree of positively correlated dependence of new risks on old risks in the portfolio, the less the improvement of spread in the event of portfolio growth will be.

This rule does not apply to negatively correlated risks, which are, however, quite rare in practice.

On the other hand the following applies:

Principle 3a

> A good improvement of spread can be achieved in a growing portfolio if the newly introduced risks are independent of each other and of the risks already covered in the existing portfolio. (An even better spread could be obtained with negatively correlated risks.)

Example 2

Let us assume that a large risk carrier has a 100 times larger share in exactly the same risks than a small carrier. His total loss and total loss fluctuation will also be 100 times higher. The loss result of the larger risk carrier is "totally dependent" on the loss result of the small risk carrier, the relative fluctuations, and the spread of risks, as well as the number of losses and the loss statistics available being the same for both risk carriers. The law of large numbers is thus not better fulfilled or utilized by the big risk carrier than by the small risk carrier.

If each share of the large risk carrier in a risk is divided into 100 small shares and these small shares are considered to be single risks, the 100 shares are totally dependent on each other. If the risk carrier distributed the 100 shares among 100 different risks which are independent of each other, as in Example 1, he would achieve a better balance of results. He would increase the number of independent risks and the expected number of losses and thus better fulfill the law of large numbers.

Principle 4

> The higher the degree of dependence of positively correlated risks on each other, the less

> the law of large numbers is fulfilled and the worse the balance in results to be expected will be.

The law of large numbers leads to the principle of spread or balance, the basic principle of any insurance activity.

According to Principles 3 and 3a, it may well happen that a risk is insurable for a certain risk carrier, because it is independent of the other risks in his portfolio, and uninsurable for another risk carrier of equal size, because it accumulates with the risks in *his* portfolio.

It can be shown that an insurer can plan all the better and be all the more competitive, the more balanced his insurance portfolio is. It is therefore a prime necessity for each risk carrier to provide for a good spread of risks (i.e., for a balanced portfolio). To achieve this goal, strict accumulation control in the case of catastrophe risks is extremely important.

Final Remark

A risk may be totally independent of any other risk or even be of an entirely random nature and still be uninsurable, because either the premium offered is too low or another criterion is not satisfied. Thus the allocation of a value equal to 0 on some insurability axis or other is not necessarily a guarantee of insurability.

On the other hand, it may still be reasonable to speak of a risk and to insure it if the exact time of occurrence of a loss is known but the loss amount that will be caused by the event remains unknown. The degree of randomness will then be equal to 0 as regards the time of occurrence, but not as regards the loss amount.

4.2 MAXIMUM POSSIBLE LOSS (MPL)

With regard to the insurability criterion MPL, it is possible to emphasize the objective or the subjective aspect. In the objective sense, maximum possible loss (or maximum probable loss or estimated maximum loss) means that which could occur in respect of a certain risk. Subjective interpretation refers to the maximum possible loss which a risk carrier will have to indemnify when covering a certain risk in whole or in part.

If a risk is entirely covered by several risk carriers, *the sum of all subjective MPLs is equal to the objective or risk-related MPL.* More generally: *The sum of the subjective risks is equal to the objective risk.* Instead of speaking of an objective risk, we can also speak of a *risk object.* Let us assume a certain risk carrier does not have enough capacity to cover a certain risk in toto but is willing and able to bear 10% of it. In the objective interpretation the risk is uninsurable for this risk carrier. The fact that he can cover 10% of the risk cannot be expressed in risk terminology unless the difficult concept of *partial insurability* is introduced. However, we want to avoid this concept, which does not fit into our simple geometric interpretation of insurability as an area. A further reason for avoiding partial insurability is the fact that it would have to be accompanied by the introduction of a *degree of partial insurability,* as it is necessary to distinguish whether a risk can be covered by a certain risk carrier up to 10% or up to 50%. Must we, therefore, as it might appear, neglect a considerable amount of information by not considering the concepts of partial insurability and the degree of partial insurability? The answer is no!

If we consider the criterion of maximum possible loss from the subjective viewpoint, we need neither introduce new concepts nor lose informative content. Ten percent and 100% cover of the same risk subjectively means two different risks for the risk carrier, for which two different points are allocated in the geometric model, one in the area of subjective insurability, one in that of subjective uninsurability.

Now the subjective interpretation can also be carried over to the objective points of view. Ten percent of a risk is accordingly no longer to be regarded as a *part of the risk,* but as a *new risk* to which perhaps a point in the objective area of insurability or in the gray zone can be assigned.

We see from the preceding considerations that subjectively considering the insurability of risks will not only be decisive in practice for the individual risk carrier, but that a certain objective interpretation also comes to the forefront in the theoretical analysis of certain insurability criteria only as a consequence of a natural subjective interpretation.

4.3 AVERAGE LOSS AMOUNT AND LOSS FREQUENCY

Insurability criteria c and d (average loss amount upon occurrence and average period of time between two loss occurrences) are closely linked and will accordingly be analyzed jointly. Let us begin with an examination which has no immediate connection with the two criteria.

4.3.1 *The Ergodic Hypothesis*

A basic principle of kinetic gas theory in physics states that the average over time is approximately equal to the average over quantity. The larger the time of observation and the quantity, the closer the averages. If we therefore carry out 1000 measurements on one molecule (or atom) over 1000 units of time, we will obtain on average a similar result as if we had made 1000 measurements on 1000 identical molecules (or atoms) in a single unit of time. It is assumed that the effects of the molecules on each other can be disregarded. This principle, known as the *ergodic hypothesis,* can be applied to insurance, where the molecules are replaced by risks.

If we have 1000 identical risks in a portfolio which are independent of each other (i.e., exert no influence on each other), and we measure the total annual loss burden or average loss per risk each year (= total loss burden : 1000), we can expect a similar result as if we had measured the total loss or average loss per year of one of these risks over a period of 1000 years. In both cases we assume each risk to be restored to its original state after each loss. Here we have of course assumed ideal conditions (which, in reality, do not exist): that we have 1000 identical, independent risks in the portfolio and that we can observe a risk for 1000 years under unchanged conditions, the risk being restored to its original state after each loss occurrence. We often try to adapt reality to such ideal conditions in statistical studies by *splitting up a portfolio into homogeneous parts*, by eradicating the effects of inflation by deflating monetary values in calculations, and so on. We can therefore take the ergodic hypothesis to be approximately valid. In insurance language it would read:

The spread over quantity (number of risks) is equal to the spread over time. The spread of 1000 identical risks over 1 year is therefore equal to the spread of 100 identical risks over 10 years, the spread of 10 identical risks over 100 years, or the "spread" of 1 risk over 1000 years.

In Section 4.1.3 attention has already been drawn to the significance of portfolio spread or balance. A further principle can be added to Principles 3, 3a, and 4 listed there.

Principle 5

> A risk carrier must seek a balance both in the number of independent risks and in time.

A risk which may be unacceptable for a risk carrier over a period of 3 months, since, if a loss occurs, no appropriate loss compensation by premium payments is subsequently possible, may be insurable for the same risk carrier over a period of 3 years (taking into account inflation).

The ergodic hypothesis leads us to the conclusion that the policy period (not to be confused with the average time interval between two loss occurrences) is a very subjective dimension of insurability, which, for simplicity's sake, has not been taken into account, but which can be subsumed under the criterion *cover limits.* In accordance with Remark B in Section 3.4 we recommend therefore that when the insurability of a risk is being assessed the period of cover be taken into account first, if it is not 1 year (which we take to be the standard case).

A disturbing factor which renders the validity of the ergodic hypothesis questionable in respect of many lines of business—at least short- or medium-term—is that of *fluctuating basic probabilities.* Normally, this factor cannot be eliminated.

Apart from inherent fluctuations, the risk is also subject to external influences which change its "risk character." Such external factors are, for example, seasonal weather conditions, which can have a great effect on motor and fire risks. Such additional risk elements appear in the form of fluctuating basic probabilities and make it impossible to observe risks under unchanged conditions as called for in the ergodic hypothesis.

It can be dangerous to assume numerous short-term risks at a time when the risk objects are strongly subject to unfavorable external circumstances; to seek a spread over the number of risks alone can have disastrous consequences under such conditions. If, on the other hand, the risks can be covered over a longer term (i.e., over several fluctuation periods of the basic probabilities), it is then possible to achieve a good balance. Principle 5 retains its validity.

Principle 6

> When building up and extending a balanced portfolio, attention must definitely be paid to fluctuating basic probabilities.

The geometric model for the two criteria *average loss amount* and *average period of time between two loss occurrences* leads to the obvious:

Principle 7

> A risk is generally the more insurable the smaller the average loss upon occurrence and the higher the loss frequency.

According to the ergodic hypothesis the balance for catastrophe risks with a large accumulation hazard, enormous sums insured, large average losses, and low loss frequency can and must be sought in time. Such catastrophe risks can then only be made insurable if the risk carriers are given the opportunity to build up long-term loss reserves from their premium income. The insurability of catastrophe risks is here related to the whole market in accordance with Section 3.4, Remark E.

4.3.2 *Loss Frequency and the Law of Large Numbers*

In Section 4.1.3 we referred to the law of large numbers and saw that it leads to the principle of spread. The misconception is often encountered that a portfolio is the more balanced the larger it is and the more risks it contains. The law of large numbers is, however, only applicable to the *number of losses.* Not only the number of risks but also the loss frequency is of importance for portfolio balance. This gives:

Principle 8

> A portfolio is the more balanced, the more losses caused by risks in the portfolio (per year)

are expected (and not necessarily the more risks there are in the portfolio).

A portfolio of 100 risks with an average loss frequency per risk of 2 (two losses per year) is therefore more balanced than a portfolio of 200 risks with an average loss frequency per risk of ½ (one loss every 2 years). In the first portfolio we expect 200 losses annually (on average) and in the second portfolio only 100 losses per year. The risks in the first portfolio have on average a loss frequency which is four times greater than that of the risks in the second portfolio and are therefore more insurable according to Principle 7. On the *d*-axis they are closer to zero.

4.3.3 *Risk Behavior of the Population*

We can conceive of each insured a priori as the self-insurer of his own risks, from which he has those risks which he cannot bear alone covered by a professional risk carrier against payment of a premium. Each self-insurer has his area of insurability and uninsurability. As studies by Kunreuther, Tversky, Kahneman, Slovic, Fischhoff, Lichtenstein, Corrigan, Combs, and others have shown, test persons often make decisions on intuition which are inconsistent with the principles we have laid out. People are often not aware at all of their true insurance needs.

The main results of their studies are:

1. People tend to cover themselves against risks with a high loss frequency and low average loss amount rather than against risks with a low loss frequency and high average loss amount.
2. If the probability of a loss sinks below a certain individually variable threshold value, people no longer show any interest whatsoever in insurance.

> This threshold value, incidentally, is almost always at a point where insurance would still be recommendable on purely objective grounds.

A natural explanation for such conduct is the fact that many people not only consider insurance to be a means of protection against possible serious losses, but also a business transaction. They want to receive within a "reasonable" period of time something in return for the premiums they have paid, ergo the tendency to insure risks with a high loss frequency.

A further explanation is the fundamentally optimistic attitude of people who question the need to protect themselves against catastrophes which only affect few victims. They tend to minimize the hazard of rare occurrences and are not prepared to pay even a minimum premium to cover such hazards; consequently they build up frequency barriers. If possible winnings rather than losses are involved, people tend to reverse this mode of behavior, as the great success of various lotteries proves, confirming the basically optimistic attitude which human beings display according to the studies in question.

We see that rational ways of acting, such as those that can be deduced from Principle 7, often contradict observed human behavior. The professional risk carrier should therefore not only try to induce the public to act rationally, but should also ensure that he sets up his own reinsurance program rationally, and not only on the basis of feeling, that he heeds insurability criteria, carefully analyzes them, and draws correct conclusions.

4.3.4 *The Effect of Reinsurance on the Area of Insurability*

Each professional risk carrier will be at pains to set up a reinsurance program in such a way that he can

1. Achieve as balanced a portfolio as possible.
2. Satisfy as many of his clients' needs as possible.

Suitable participation of other risk carriers in his risks, either as pool members, coinsurers, or reinsurers, can help the risk carrier to form his area of insurability in a favorable way. An advantageous application of the various coinsurance and reinsurance tools is therefore one of the most important aspects of his business policy. We shall refer in what follows only to reinsurance since, from the point of view of risk theory, coinsurance or pool participation can be considered as particular (usually proportional) forms of reinsurance.

At this point we should like to touch on one important aspect of reinsurance. By means of reinsurance, whether proportional or nonporportional, the average loss and the maximum possible loss are reduced for the risk carrier. In almost all forms of reinsurance, the loss frequency remains unchanged. Certain risks which are uninsurable for the risk carrier without reinsurance become subjectively insurable. Reinsurance thus increases the number and variety of potentially insurable risks for the risk carrier. According to the subjective risk interpretation given in Section 4.2, which enabled us to eliminate the concept of partial insurability, reinsurance creates *subjectively new risks* for the risk carrier.

The reduction of the average loss and the MPL releases *cover capacity*, which can be used to cover new risks. The claims frequency of new risks can be added to the unchanged claims frequency of the original risks. In this way reinsurance directly brings about a reduction of the average loss (provided the free capacity is not used for unreasonably high net commitments per risk) and indirectly increases the loss frequency in the risk carrier's portfolio. The spread of the portfolio is therefore improved in accordance with Principles 7 and 8. This improvement can be all the more pronounced the more cover capacity is released by means of reinsurance. With better portfolio spread, the risk carrier can in principle increase his area of subjective insurability. We deduce from this:

Principle 9

> A risk carrier who is willing to pay a reinsurance premium P should choose a form of rein-

surance such that, by means of premium P, as much cover capacity is released for him as possible.

Principle 9 is an important criterion, but not the only one, which has to be taken into account when choosing the best form of reinsurance.

The released cover capacity can be defined in various ways. We understand it to be that amount of money which the risk carrier would have to pay out (as dividends or otherwise) to increase the ruin probability reduced as a consequence of reinsurance to its original position.

As indicated, we want, however, to assume that this amount is used to cover new risks.

How can a reinsurance cover be best used in structuring the portfolio? Let us call a risk which we expect to produce a loss once a year *an annual risk*. A risk which we expect to produce two losses a year is equal to two annual risks, and one which is expected to produce a loss every two years to half an annual risk.

As risks with a higher loss frequency contribute more to the portfolio balance (Principle 8) than risks with a low loss frequency, and new risks independent of the portfolio bring about more balance than new risks which accumulate with the portfolio (Principle 3), we can state:

Principle 10

A risk carrier can use the capacity released by reinsurance all the better to balance his portfolio (and often also to increase his net premium) the more new annual risks he accepts which are independent of each other and of the annual risks already included in his portfolio.

Principle 10 is a more precise statement of Principle 3a.

Apart from released capacity, a risk carrier must take into consideration his own portfolio structure and the market conditions which determine how much capacity he can still put to good use; these are important factors in deciding how much reinsurance premium he is prepared to spend.

4.4 INSURANCE PREMIUM

When analyzing the insurability criterion *insurance premium*, we shall only incidentally consider the loadings contained in the premium for acquisition, agent's commission, claims handling, and administrative and miscellaneous expenses, but rather concentrate on that part of the premium required solely for cover of the risk. We shall call this part of the premium the *risk premium* and the remainder the *expense loading.*

In general, it can be said that the area of insurability of a professional risk carrier and his competitiveness are all the more limited, the greater the premiums are which he needs to cover individual risks, whether it be that his capacity is low, that he has an unbalanced portfolio, that he pursues a cautious business policy, or that he does not work efficiently (high administrative expenses, complicated claims settlement, etc.).

4.4.1 *The Pure Risk Premium and the Fluctuation Loading*

The pure risk premium is that part of the insurance premium with which the expected loss must be paid. *The pure risk premium is therefore equal to the expected annual loss.* This is calculated from criteria c and d and is equal to the expected number of losses per year, multiplied by the average loss amount on occurrence.

Example:

A risk A which is expected to produce a loss on average of 10,000,000 every 100 years would require the same pure risk premium of 100,000 = 1/100 • 10,000,000 as a risk B (or a small portfolio) expected to produce 100 losses with an average amount of 1000 per year (100,000 = 100 • 1000). Of course, risk B contributes much more to the portfolio's balance than risk A, in accordance with Principle 8. Expressed conversely, risk A contributes greatly to the imbalance of the whole portfolio and is therefore *much more dangerous* than risk B. Faced with the choice of whether to cover risk A or risk B for the same risk premium, the professional risk carrier will surely choose risk B. Risk A would only be attractive if the risk carrier received a considerable *risk loading* to compensate for the dangerousness of the risk. The risk loading would have to be large enough to make it appear worthwhile to the risk carrier to assume risk A and the consequently increased imbalance for his whole portfolio. Such a risk loading moves the risk downward on the e-axis (where the reciprocal of the insurance premium is plotted) toward the origin, from the subjective area of uninsurability into the subjective area of insurability.

Risk B is subject to potential result fluctuations (albeit considerably smaller ones than risk A), which should be compensated by a small risk loading or *fluctuation loading.* We deduce:

Principle 11

> The risk premium must contain a risk or fluctuation loading in addition to the pure risk premium.

In the literature and in practice, very often the distinction drawn between risk premium and pure risk premium is not sufficiently clear. Unfortunately, no unambiguous terminology has become generally accepted, and the pure risk premium is often referred to simply as "risk premium."

The significance of Principle 11 is underlined by the following finding arrived at mathematically. In risk theory it can be shown that, if the risk premium has no fluctuation loading for any of the insured objects, then sooner or later the risk carrier will be ruined.

In the geometric model this fact means that, leaving administrative and other nonrisk expenses aside, a premium equal to the pure risk premium should already be in the objective area of uninsurability, since, according to Principle 11, no risk should be covered by any risk carrier at such a premium. A minimal premium increase (i.e., the introduction of a minimal risk loading) would shift balanced risks into the subjective area of insurability for certain risk carriers.

To form a uniform crossover into the area of uninsurability for all risks, we shall not express the insurance premium, as in Section 3.2, in units of money but as a multiple of the pure risk premium. The insurance premium can still assume all values from zero to infinity, and we can still plot our values on the *e*-axis (1 ÷ insurance premium), where the point 1 should lie in the subjective area of uninsurability of each risk carrier.

Remark 1

Introducing such a complicated unit as the "pure risk premium" in Section 3.2 would have been confusing. At that point we therefore expressed the insurance premium in units of money, which as more thorough analysis now shows is impractical.

The expenses of all types cannot be determined in advance with certainty. They are a random quantity just as the risk premium is. If the actual expenses incurred prove to be smaller than the expense loading, then the risk carrier makes an *expense profit*. In the opposite case, he suffers a loss. Just as we consider the pure risk premium as the expected annual claim, so we can define an *expected* expense loading as the expected value of the random quantity "expenses." We can now elaborate on Principle 11: The pure risk premium plus the expected loading for expenses *should* be in the subjective area of uninsurability for each risk carrier.

In reality the subjective area of uninsurability sometimes begins at higher values on the e-axis, since there are risk carriers who will cover risks for commercial reasons even against premiums which are lower than the pure risk premium plus the expected loading for expenses. Such reasons can arise from competitive considerations, such as the wish to gain entry into a given market or to consolidate an existing market position. They can also result from long-term planning considerations; it may appear wise to assume the cover of certain risks for a certain period on an underrated basis or to accept specific underrated risks in order to retain or acquire other, more desirable business connected with them.

We shall from now on ignore the expenses, with a few exceptions.

Remark 2

Throughout the text we generally disregard the considerable importance of premium and loss reserves, their run-off and investment, as well as the impact of inflation and foreign exchange fluctuations so as not to become diverted from our main subject or led into the particular problems of specific lines of business.

To compare dangerousness of risks A and B in our last example and to show how portfolio imbalances can drastically increase the probability of ruin, let us expand the example somewhat. If we assume that the risk carrier has at his disposal free reserves of 5 million and that he can increase his free reserves (not premium and loss reserves) annually by 50,000 on average, then the occurrence of a loss of 10 million at some point of time within the next 100 years would, with high probability, bring about his ruin. With a planning horizon of 100 years, the probability of ruin due to risk A is therefore very great. On the other hand, it is very improbable that an annual loss caused by risk B will exceed 20,000. Even if a loss of 20,000 were to occur year after year 100 times, the total loss of 2 million would still only be 40% of the original free reserves of 5 million. The ruin probability over 100 years associated with risk B is thus extremely small.

We have assumed that the free reserves increase each year on average by 50,000 and therefore, indirectly, that the risk premiums for the risks in the portfolio have a built-in fluctuation loading, since pure risk premiums can, by definition, contribute nothing to the growth of the free reserves in the long run. We deduce:

Principle 12

> The risk loadings contribute on average (or, according to the ergodic hypothesis, in the long run) to the growth of the risk carrier's free reserves. They are also responsible for underwriting profits.

In our example, risk A is expected either to produce an annual loss of zero or one of 10 million. For risk B, an annual total claims amount between 80,000 and 120,000 is to be expected with high probability; in other words, much smaller fluctuations are to be expected than in the case of risk A. *Fluctuations in results are a gauge of the balance of a risk or of a portfolio.*

In the reasoning which preceded Principle 11, we saw that coverage of risk A necessitates a much greater risk loading than is the case for risk B. We can therefore deduce:

Principle 13

> The greater the potential result fluctuations of a risk, the more it contributes to the imbalance of a portfolio and to the increase of the risk carrier's ruin probability, and the higher the fluctuation loading for the cover concerned must be.

The *service rendered* by the risk carrier is much higher for the cover of risk *A* than for risk *B*. The need for a higher risk premium or higher fluctuation loading respectively for risk *A* can also be explained by the *principle of balance between supply and demand.* Given the same premium, many more risk carriers will be prepared to supply a cover for risk *B* than for risk *A*, since with this premium risk *B* will lie in the insurability area of many more risk carriers than will risk *A*. Risk *B* is more attractive than risk *A* and can be covered at a lower price on the insurance market.

Remark 3

In Chapter 2 we gave an example to illustrate the apparent incompleteness of our system of criteria and mentioned that the criterion *subjectively recognized uncertainty of risks* can be included in the criterion *insurance premium.* In Remark C, Section 3.4, we showed how, as a consequence of better information, a risk became insurable; in the example, it was not the point allocated to the risk which shifted into the subjective area of insurability, but the latter area itself was enlarged as a consequence of better information so as also to include the point in question.

Let us now imagine two risks which are independent of each other and have the same sum insured, the same expected average loss, and the same expected loss frequency; let us assume that they are free of moral hazard and that their cover is both consistent with public policy and legally permissible. Let the same premium be paid for both risks. The only difference is that we know that the first risk generates exactly one loss per year, while with the second one loss *on average* occurs per year, it being however possible for 10 loss-free years to be followed by one very heavy loss year.

The second risk is subject to greater fluctuations and is the more dangerous of the two. As the same premium is paid for both, the first risk is either overrated or the second one underrated. It is therefore conceivable that for certain risk carriers the first risk is insurable at the given premium but the second not, although both risks are mapped onto the same point in the geometric model. For those risk carriers the point would lie on the subjective boundary line. By introducing an additional criterion, which we can call *objective uncertainty of risks* or *objective fluc-*

tuation of risks, we can allocate to the two risks two different points, one of which lies in the subjective area of insurability and the other in the subjective area of uninsurability. In contrast to the previously mentioned *subjectively recognized uncertainty of risks,* the objective fluctuation criterion which is also integrated in the insurance premium criterion is independent of time and reveals a *genuine*, rather than a merely apparent, incompleteness of our system of criteria.

As the example is rather theoretical, and in practice large fluctuations are usually connected with large maximum possible and average losses and low frequencies, which could force the risk into the area of uninsurability, we have refrained for the sake of simplicity from introducing a tenth objective fluctuation dimension. A comparison of risks A and B in the example in this section illustrates the great effect of criteria b, c, and d on the fluctuations of a risk carrier's operating results.

4.4.2 *The Two Types of Safety Loadings*

We have spoken thus far of the levels of risk or fluctuation loadings needed because of the hazards associated with the risks. The amount of the risk loading, however, not only depends on the nature of the risk but also on the size and structure of the risk carrier's portfolio, the amount of his reserves, his acceptance policy, and other subjective aspects which we shall concentrate on in this section.

By assuming the cover of a risk, the risk carrier also assumes the hazards associated with it. He burdens himself with a certain uncertainty for the future and must therefore be recompensed by an *uncertainty loading.* According to Principle 12, this loading also accords him a certain degree of safety and is therefore also called a *safety loading*. It is also possible to say that the risk carrier provides the insured with security by assuming the uncertainty to which the insured is subject for the price of a safety or uncertainty loading. The subjective portfolio-related terminology for the concept "fluctuation loading" would therefore be *safety* or *uncertainty loading.*

When setting the fluctuation loading, the risk carrier must take into account two types of safety loadings. The *first* *loading, Z_1, would stem from the uncertainty in the estimation of the expected total loss; the second loading, Z_2, would be intended as compensation for covering the hazards inherent in the risk.* Uncertainty in the estimation of the expected total loss is closely connected with the problem of information, which we already came across in the example at the end of Chapter 2. This immediately gives rise to the question of the *calculability* of risk premiums.

How should the premium for catastrophe risks be determined when there is no or only very little claims information available? How is the reinsurer to determine the premium for an excess of loss cover on a very high layer that has never been affected by a loss in the past?

Risks of this type often lie in the dark gray zone. For various risk carriers they can, under certain circumstances, be moved into the area of insurability by applying the following measures:

1. Procuring and evaluating loss material from similar risks and related lines of business.
2. Procuring and evaluating nonloss material which is important for evaluating the risk (e.g., seismological and geological data to assess an earthquake risk). Particular attention should be paid to the possible loss potential and to the *potential* (as opposed to the *observed*) loss fluctuations.
3. Evaluation of statistical laws and mathematical models (e.g., adaptation of an analytical loss function to the known loss material in low layers and extrapolation of this function into the high layers where no loss experience is available).

With means such as these, which will increase the risk carrier's administrative expenses slightly, the loading Z_1, can be reduced. Risks formerly judged as underrated on the basis of intuition can be revalued, and the original premium under certain circumstances may be found to be appropriate.

These clarifying measures may, however, have the reverse effect and prove certain premiums judged to be adequate to be in fact unsuitable. In such a case the risk carrier contracts his subjective area of insurability. Such clarification can be of utmost importance, as too generous an acceptance policy based on a lack of experience has already proved disastrous for many a risk carrier.

The importance of information for the risk carrier is obvious. If already available information on a risk is not conveyed to the risk carrier, deliberately or otherwise, this additional lack of information must lead to an increase of the safety loading Z_1. Shortage of information increases the risk element for the risk carrier and reduces the calculability of the risk premium and the possibility of correctly assessing the risk.

From the remarks made so far we can summarize the following points:

1. The subjective insurability of a risk not only depends on the nature (hazardousness) and size of the risk, portfolio composition, and acceptance policy of the risk carrier, but also on the extent of the information to which the risk carrier has access.
2. *Inadequate information* increases the insecurity factor and *justifies higher security loadings.*
3. *Better-than-average information should be rewarded* in certain cases with a bonus, in analogy to fire protection measures in fire insurance.
4. *If the information furnished by the insured is sparse, the security which the insured receives from an objective viewpoint is less than the insecurity which the risk carrier assumes from a subjective viewpoint!* This lack of information could be justified if it were too costly to acquire the information (i.e., if doing so would cost more than the premium surcharge caused by the lack of information).

If the security loading Z_1 can be reduced by improving the information on the risk and the assessment thereof, the security loading Z_2 based on the hazardousness of the risk can be reduced by decreasing this hazardousness. The latter can only be achieved by measures applied to the risk itself. Here one thinks for example of the sprinkler system in fire insurance or, where the human element is important in the risk, as in motor insurance, of measures such as increasing retention or introducing a bonus–malus system based on loss experience.

As the number of hazardous risks which are difficult to assess is constantly growing and the need for cover of new, previously unknown or disregarded risk categories (e.g., environmental liability) arises ever more frequently, *risk management* has gained in importance in recent years, and there has been an enormous upsurge of interest in those aspects of *mathematical risk theory* which can be usefully put into practice. Both risk theory and risk management, however, can and must be developed further.

Principle 14

> In our attempts to obtain and evaluate claims material and other information and to apply risk theory and risk management, we should pursue the goal of making as many risks as possible insurable on the one hand, and of identifying risks which under certain conditions are *not* insurable (e.g., underrated ones) on the other.

We can now further analyze the example in Section 4.4.1: Both risks, A and B, have an identical expected annual loss of 100,000 (over an average of many years), risk A being, however, much more dangerous than risk B. It is also to be assumed that the uncertainty as to whether the expected annual loss has in fact been correctly estimated at 100,000 is much greater in respect of risk A than of risk B (we claimed to know for example that with risk A a loss of 10 million could be expected on average every 100 years). The pure risk premium of 100,000 is the same for both risks, but both components Z_1 and Z_2 of the security loading are much higher for risk A than for risk B. In fact, the safety loading for risk B will only need to be a *fraction* of the pure risk premium to be considered appropriate by most risk carriers. On the other hand, risk A will only lie in the area of insurability for most risk carriers, if at all, if the safety loading is a *multiple* of the pure risk premium.

Remark 1

Just as the degree of randomness can be described by the mathematically strictly defined concept of correlation coefficient (Section 4.1.1), the result fluctuations of a risk or portfolio can also be exactly defined by various mathematical concepts. The most useful and most frequently employed concept for measuring fluctuation potential is the *standard deviation.*

Remark 2

Theoretical considerations show that the information-related safety loading Z_1 should be proportional to the standard deviation, whereas the risk-related safety loading Z_2 should be proportional to the square of the standard deviation, which we call *variance.* This fact reflects the fundamentally different nature of these two types of loadings, both of which should be taken into consideration in the rating.

Remark 3

Let us call the standard deviation of a risk or portfolio relative to the risk premium income the *relative standard deviation.* The relative standard deviation can serve as a useful gauge in assessing the balance of a portfolio (see Example 1 in Section 4.1.3).

Remark 4

We have broken the criterion *insurance premium* into three parts, the pure risk premium, which can be determined by criteria c and d, the safety loading, of which we distinguished and analyzed two types, and the expense loading.

4.4.3 *Risk Premium and Utility Theory*

> *"What is wealth? For some people an old shirt is already wealth. Others are poor with ten millions."*
>
> Franz Kafka

The *utility function, u,* is a basic concept of economics. What is essential for an individual or a company is not so much an amount of money, an article, or a service in itself, but the subjective *value,* the *utility,* attached to the amount of money, article, or service by the individual or company. The value of a particular object can be variously interpreted depending on the circumstances. A thousand monetary units (say, for example, dollars, pounds, DM, or francs) will have less value for a rich man than for a poor man. Each (real or corporate) person decides subjectively what value he attached to the first, second, or tenth thousand units of accumulated capital and by so doing fixes a subjective utility function.

The form of the utility function can reveal much about a person's generosity and attitude toward risk or about a company's business practices. The mode of conduct shown by a person in the way he handles his financial affairs, which we could describe as miserly, generous, or wasteful, determines the value which he attaches to a unit of money. A utility function is nothing more than an expression of this conduct set out quantitatively in a formula which is dependent on wealth. Naturally, an individual or the decision-making bodies of a company are not necessarily aware of the existence of a utility function reflecting their conduct, just as a person need not take notice of a mirror in which his every movement is in fact reflected.

To be sure, if the person looks into the mirror he becomes aware of his external appearance and can then pay greater attention to it. Similarly, knowledge of the utility function can make it easier for an individual or company to establish sound business principles and decision criteria. We want to draw the consequences of the utility theory for a risk carrier, his premium structure and area of insurability.

We have seen that different people attach different importance to the first, second, or tenth thousand units of income or savings. Two general behavior patterns can, however, be observed:

Behavior Pattern 1

Each of the thousand units of money must have a positive utility value; otherwise, it would be given away.

Behavior Pattern 2

The first thousand units are more important than the second, which in turn are more important than the third, and so on. An annual salary increase from 10,000 to 11,000 will be more important than one from 100,000 to 101,000.

Accordingly, a utility function will be increasing; the marginal growth in utility will, however, decrease with increasing income or assets. These characteristics are shown graphically in Figure 6.

Example

Let us assume that an investor has invested 10,000 out of a capital of 11,000 in a promising project, to which he attaches a utility value of 12,000. He has kept 1000 in cash. There is a 5% probability of the project failing, in which case the whole of the 10,000 investment would be lost. The investor would like to protect himself against this eventuality. If the risk carrier asks for a premium of 1000 for the cover (i.e., 10% of the cover amount), the investor will buy the cover, because his 1000 in cash, according to Figure 6, has a utility value of only 240 for him (i.e., 2% of the project utility of 12,000). With 2% of the project utility he can protect himself against a 5% probability of loss. Viewed objectively, the pure risk premium is of course 5% of the cover amount. The risk carrier therefore receives twice the pure risk premium as his charge for providing cover. If we assume that expenses are minimal, the fluctuation loading is almost 100% of the

Figure 6

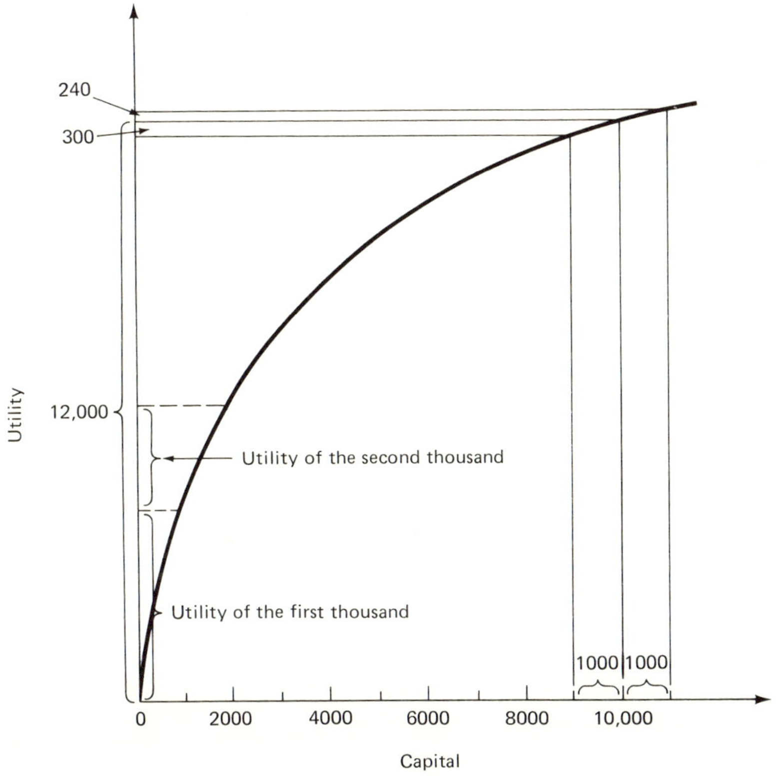

pure risk premium, which could in general be regarded by the risk carrier as a high loading. It therefore appears favorable for investor and risk carrier alike to enter into this arrangement for coverage of the risk.

Let us now vary the example:

First Variant

Let us assume the investor possesses a capital of 10,100, of which 1000 is invested in a project and 9100 retained in cash. There is a 5% probability that the 1000 could be lost. Would this investor (assuming the same utility function as before) also be prepared to insure the project against a premium of 10% of the cover amount, that is, 100 units of money? As the utility curve flattens off somewhat, the 100 monetary units between 10,000 and 10,100 for the premium will, according to Figure 6, have a utility value of more than 24, and the loss of the 1000 units invested in the project would be equal to the importance of the loss of 300 units (= utility of the 1000 units between 9000 and 10,000). For a loss probability of 5%, the investor would have to pay a "utility premium" of more than 8% (24 ÷ 300). This cover would be too expensive for the investor, as the loss of 1000 monetary units (or 300 utility units) would not hit him too hard.

Second Variant

Let us now assume the figures in Figure 6 to be in *thousands* of monetary units and the utility function to be that of a risk carrier. Let his capital be 10 million monetary units. Would he be prepared to assume a risk which has a 5% probability of producing a loss of 10 million monetary units against a premium of 1 million units? Here the risk carrier would have to risk the loss of his entire capital with a 5% probability in return for a premium which would present 2% of his capital utility—a bad deal. For the risk carrier, a safety loading of almost 100% of the pure risk premium would not be enough to cover this large risk, which would plunge the portfolio of the risk carrier into too great a state of imbalance. By large risk we mean one which has a high sum insured or large MPL.

We summarize:

In the example, the risk carrier could have obtained and would have accepted the cover of a risk of 10,000 monetary units with a loss occurrence probability of 5% against a fluctuation loading of almost 100% of the pure risk premium. In the first variant, he would not have obtained a risk with the same probability of loss occurrence, but with a cover amount of only 1000 monetary units, unless he had drastically reduced the fluctuation loading below 100% of the pure risk premium. In the second variant, the risk carrier would not have accepted a large risk with the same loss occurrence probability, but a cover amount of 10 million monetary units, against a fluctuation loading of 100% of the pure risk premium. Depending on the utility function, he would have been prepared to cover only a part of the large risk (e.g., 1%).

We deduce:

Principle 15

> The larger the risk carrier's participation in the cover of a large risk, the more the fluctuation loading must increase in relation to the pure risk premium.

The increasing share of the safety loading in the total premium with increasing commitment can be interpreted as *price for the additional capacity.* Principle 15 is a generalized formulation of the "price for capacity" principle worked out by G. Benktander.

It is also possible to define a *risk aversion* based on the utility function. Insurance contracts, such as those described in the example, are concluded when the risk aversion of the insured is so much greater than that of the professional risk carrier that the insured is prepared to get rid of a risk in return for a premium which is in turn large enough to make the risk carrier overcome his risk aversion.

In accordance with behavior pattern 2, a risk carrier will feel the loss of 1 million *more* than 10 times as much as the loss of 100,000. Only an appropriate "price for capacity" will overcome his increasing risk aversion. If the premium asked for is too high for the insured in the end, the risk falls into the risk carrier's subjective area of uninsurability.

Fixing the utility function depending on reserves, portfolio composition, business policy, and so on, means already making a great contribution in marking out the insurability limits of a risk carrier.

Remark

In the example in Chapter 2 illustrating criteria not satisfied independently and conditionally, we assumed an absolute upper limit L for a risk carrier's commitment per event. Let us suppose that the MPL of a certain risk object is L. In the example the risk carrier would have been prepared to cover 5% ($= L/20$) but not 10% ($=L/10$) of the risk object for a premium of P. If we express the premium in units of money, as originally envisaged, such a situation is easy to imagine. In Section 4.4.1, however, we saw how useful it can be to express the insurance premium as a multiple of the pure risk premium.

Is the preceding example still valid? The insurance premium is "equally large" in units of the pure risk premium if it is twice as large in units of money for the cover of 10% of L as for the cover of 5% of L. Since, according to Principle 15, the cover of 10% of L should cost more than twice as much as the cover of 5% of L, it is quite possible for the situation assumed in the example (that 5% but not 10% of L can be covered by a premium P) to occur, even if P is expressed as a multiple of the pure risk premium rather than in units of money.

Similar considerations lead to the conclusion that Example 3 in Section 3.3 also requires no modification.

4.4.4 *The Insurance Premium for Similarly Structured Objects of Various Sizes*

Example

Let us imagine two similarly structured factories which produce the same product and have taken the same fire protection measures, which differ, however, in size. One factory has an insurance value of 1 million monetary units, the other factory of 10 million. Let the owner of the smaller factory pay a premium of 2‰. Should now the owner of the larger factory pay the same premium rate, a lower, or a higher one for the same cover?

A businessman might think right away of a quantity rebate and be prepared to rate the larger factory at a lower premium rate. For similar reasons, dazzled by the considerably greater premium income in monetary units, many a risk carrier will grant the owner of the larger factory a discount with a side glance at the competition. In our example, this would be a wrong decision, as numerous statistical and theoretical studies have shown for similar situations.

When covering the ten times larger factory, the premium rate should rather be increased, and the factory owner loaded with an *antidiscount*. There are several reasons for this:

First Reason

To judge from the available statistical studies, the expected annual total loss (i.e., the pure risk premium) is more than ten times larger in the case of the large factory than in that of the smaller one. Although the average loss relative to the sum insured in the large factory will be lower than in the smaller factory, this advantage will usually be more than offset by the much higher loss frequency to be expected in the large factory. With many more workers and perhaps ten times more machinery or larger, more complicated and more sensitive machinery, the danger elements which could cause a loss occurrence are greatly increased.

In the preceding example, we included the possibility of partial losses and of various loss frequencies, in other words risk elements which we disregarded in the section on utility theory, to which topic we shall now briefly return.

Second Reason

As we have seen in the first reason, the pure risk premium for the cover of 10% of the large factory will be larger than the pure risk premium for the cover of 100% of the smaller factory. This difference between the pure risk premiums will, however, be at least partially offset by a smaller safety loading for the cover of 10% of the large factory as a consequence of its greater balance (greater loss frequency, law of large numbers, Principle 8).

Even if we assume the premiums for the smaller factory and for 10% of the larger factory to be equal, the premium rate to cover 100% of the large factory would have to increase considerably according to utility theory and Principle 15!

Third Reason

Imagine that the large factory could be divided up into ten small ones, as shown in Figure 7, each of which is identical with the small factory shown on the left. If the ten factories are separated from each other by fire walls in such a way that no loss occurrence can spread from one factory to the others, then the pure risk premium for the cover of the ten factories must be ten times as large as that for the cover of one factory, but the safety loading less than ten times as large because of the greater balance. If we now dispense with the imaginary fire walls, a large accumulation hazard is created, in addition to the other existing risks, the cover of which necessitates a corresponding additional premium charge. This additional premium charge should generally be larger than the above-mentioned reduction of the safety loading as a result of greater balance. Cover for the large factory therefore costs more than ten times that of the small factory.

Of course, risk objects are never identical and usually not even similar, and it can definitely occur that when all insurability dimensions are taken into account, a large object at a

Figure 7

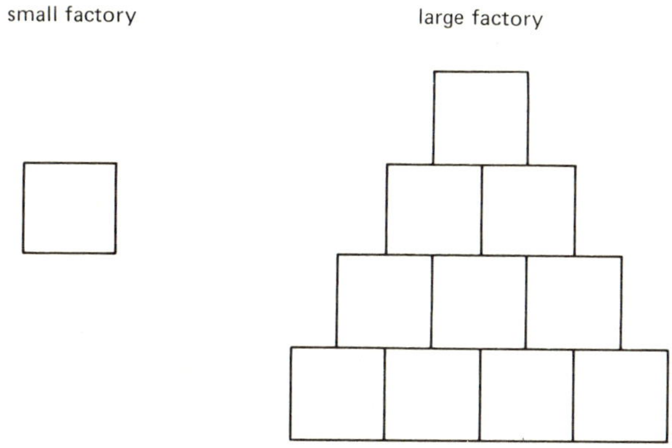

certain premium rate still lies within the subjective area of insurability of a risk carrier, while a much smaller object at the same premium rate must be considered as an uninsurable risk by the same risk carrier.

If we concentrate, however, on the size factor of the risk object, we can say:

Principle 16

> **With growing MPL or sum insured, the premium rate should also grow (antidiscount principle).**

Adhering to Principle 16 can protect the risk carrier from unpleasant surprises. If the principle is not heeded, the risk carrier will set a wrong subjective insurability area. He grants premium discounts on major risks, which should only be brought into the subjective area of insurability against much higher premiums.

In a competitive climate in which a risk carrier wants to retain his market share, it is not always simple to adhere to Principle 16. Once "principle breakers" grant premium discounts on high sums insured, they can sometimes induce the whole insurance market to follow suit. Reasonable business practices only return when the price has been paid for ill-considered practices of this kind. Only then are subjective insurability areas adapted again to risk carriers' real circumstances.

As general adherence to principles such as Principle 16 can be shaken by some few "principle breakers," there exists an *unstable equilibrium* in a freely competitive insurance market which is a cause of the major premium fluctuations in time in the insurance industry, especially for the cover of large risks.

Remark 1

Principle 16 is quantitatively less precise but more general than Principle 15.

Whereas various *cover participations* were compared for the same risk object in Principle 15, the comparison is extended in Principle 16 to various *risk objects*.

Remark 2

By expanding and modernizing a production unit, increased efficiency and profitability can be expected. The resulting increase in premium rate according to Principle 16 should be taken into consideration and paid for out of increased profits by the insured.

Remark 3

If part of the modernization of a plant is devoted to the reduction of its susceptibility to loss and accident, this should be rewarded by a corresponding premium reduction.

Remark 4

In the discussion which led to Principle 16, we ignored the expense loading. However, the *expense rate* is dependent upon the size of the risk and in general decreases as the latter increases but never falls to 0%. With increasing size of the risk the *commission rate related to sum insured* either remains constant or also decreases toward an *asymptotic commission rate* (see Figure 8). On the other hand, the relative risk loading (anti-discount) must rise steadily with increasing risk size. Principle 16 therefore retains its validity, at least from a certain risk size G on (see Figure 8).

Figure 8

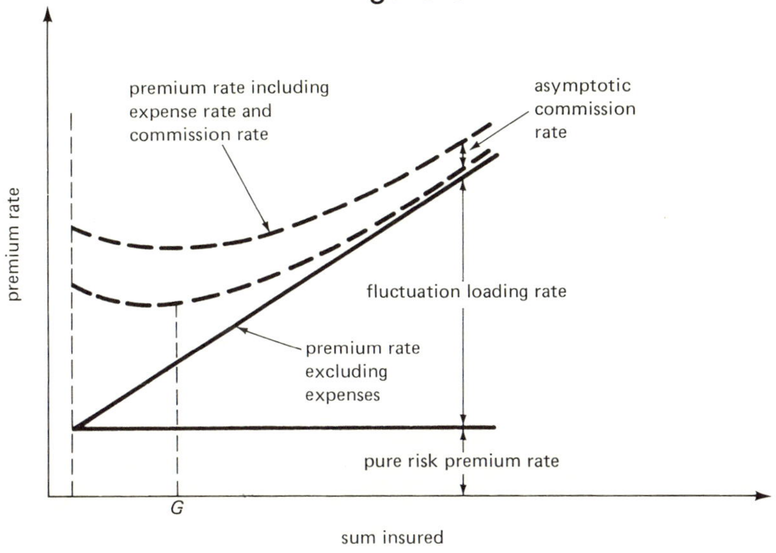

4.4.5 *Reinsurance Cover and Reinsurance Premium*

If a risk carrier cannot cover a large risk alone, he will cover that part of it which lies within his subjective area of insurability, provided he can find a suitable reinsurer to cover the rest. The size of the part retained by the risk carrier depends on the premium offered, the free reserves, the utility function, the type of reinsurance, and the reinsurance premium.

For the sake of simplicity, let us now consider a quota-share treaty, although similar considerations could also be made and corresponding conclusions drawn for any other form of reinsurance. Evidently, a retained percentage of the cover of a large risk is all the more likely to border on the subjective area of uninsurability of a risk carrier, the lower the premium offered, the higher the reinsurance premium (i.e., the lower the commission) and the smaller the free reserves.

The lower the overall premium offered for the cover of a large risk, the greater the share which the risk carrier will have to reinsure. The reinsurer, himself a risk carrier, will, however, according to Principle 15, also have to increase his reinsurance premium the greater his share. As the total premium decreases, the point will ultimately be reached where either the ceding company can no longer keep a fixed minimum retention within its subjective area of insurability or else the part to be reinsured moves out of the reinsurer's area of insurability. The large risk then cannot be fully covered by the insurer and reinsurer together. The possibility then exists of either partly covering the major risk or of increasing the premium rate or of calling in other reinsurers.

On the other hand, the party seeking cover has the possibility of depressing the cover price for his risk for as long as it takes to use the full market capacity (i.e., to involve all interested risk carriers). The price becomes minimal when all interested risk carriers have to advance to the limit of uninsurability with their share at the price offered so that the risk can just be fully covered. Should the price offered be below this minimum price, the risk would lie in the objective area of uninsurability.

If the risk is oversubscribed at a certain price, then a lower price could have been achieved. A risk is all the more easy to oversubscribe, the more risk carriers are interested in the cover. The higher the price, the more interesting the cover and the larger the elbowroom for the broker. To expand the circle of risk carriers is not worthwhile if the work this entails is costlier than the premium reduction that still can be achieved.

We have now dealt with the insurance and reinsurance of a major risk, while in Section 4.3.4 we studied the effect of a reinsurance cover on a whole portfolio. If reinsurance commission (in percentage of the reinsurance premium) is larger than the expenses (in percentage of the overall premium), then quota-share reinsurance results in an expense profit. By partly dispensing with this profit, the risk carrier can reduce premiums and increase his competitiveness.

Quota-share reinsurance leaves the relative standard deviation of a risk or portfolio defined in Remark 3, Section 4.4.2, unchanged. The relative standard deviation of a risk is likewise not changed by a surplus reinsurance cover. In general, the relative standard deviation of a portfolio is reduced for the ceding company as the result of a surplus reinsurance cover, that of a risk or of a portfolio by an excess of loss cover, and that of a portfolio by a stop loss cover. The reduction in the relative standard deviation is often particularly marked in the case of non-proportional forms of reinsurance. This reduction makes possible reductions in safety margins (i.e., in direct insurance premiums), and therefore improves the competitiveness of the reinsured risk carrier.

As a result of Sections 4.3.4 and 4.4.5, we can summarize:

Principle 17

> As a consequence of suitable reinsurance covers, a risk carrier can increase the number of risks in his area of insurability, often reduce the relative standard deviation, further balance his portfolio, increase his competitiveness, expand his acceptance policy, and enlarge his expense profit.

4.5 MORAL HAZARD

4.5.1 *Determining the Problem*

The previously analyzed criteria can be mathematically described and evaluated. We have been able to distinguish and analyze characteristics linked to the risk object and characteristics linked to the risk carrier and to ascertain a direct connection between risk object and risk carrier.

On three occasions we have also examined the party seeking cover. In Section 4.4.3 we saw that the decision whether a party will seek cover for a risk object, and, if so, at what conditions, depends on his utility function and the value which he attaches to the loss of a risk object. At several points we indicated the significance of the applicant for cover as supplier of information on the risk to be covered. Finally, in Section 4.4.2 we mentioned the case where the applicant himself is part of the risk (the example was motor insurance).

In the following section we shall primarily deal with the owner of the risk seeking to pass on the risk against payment of a premium; here the owner is not himself part of the risk but constitutes an *additional risk element.* We shall extend our comments to parties who are not identical with the owner of the risk but who are involved in some way as additional risk elements.

The relationship "risk object—risk carrier" is to be extended in our considerations of risks to a multiple relationship, "risk object—risk owner—other parties involved as additional risk elements—risk carrier."

All considerations in Sections 4.1 to 4.4 were built on the assumption that the *sole motivation of the applicant for cover was protection against the consequences of a potential loss occurrence.* It was simply a case of probing hazards inherent in the risks.

With the criterion of moral hazard, which has no obvious expression in terms of mathematics and risk theory, we want to include parties who perhaps have motives for seeking insurance *other than* protection against losses. When such parties exist and cause at least one risk carrier to reject the cover of a risk, we say that such risk is *morally hazardous.*

In Section 3.2 we let moral hazard in the objective interpretation, which we also call *degree of moral hazard*, assume the values 0, $1/N$, $2/N$, . . ., $(N-2)/N$, $(N-1)/N$, $N/N = 1$, where N was the number of all risk carriers. The degree of moral hazard n/N was assumed if n of the N risk carriers would refuse a risk because they did not regard the criterion moral hazard as being either independently or conditionally satisfied. The value 0 lay on the f-axis in the objective area of insurability, the value 1 in the objective area of uninsurability, and all other values in the gray zone. Formerly we defined the moral hazard of risks in terms of the conduct of risk carriers. Would it not be more reasonable and practical to take the parties who are the cause of the moral hazard, or more precisely their *intentions,* as the gauge of moral hazard? We shall answer this question in Section 4.5.3.

4.5.2 *Deliberate Intervention in a Risk*

A risk can be *intentionally affected* by the act of some party. We can discern two principal modes of conduct, which are different both in time and usually also in intention, motivation, and effect. In one case, the act is carried out *before* the conclusion of an insurance policy, in the other case, *afterward.* Intervention in a risk prior to conclusion of a policy usually aims at preventing a loss, subsequent intervention usually at provoking one.

If a party intervenes in the risk to be covered before cover has been obtained, this is usually with the intention to reduce in his own interest the danger of a loss occurrence and the expected pecuniary loss following a loss occurrence on the one hand and, on the other hand, to reduce the risk premium. (After conclusion of the policy, the latter motive no longer exists.) The risk carrier should encourage such preventive measures on the part of the applicant for cover and his interest in "his risk" by means of premium rebates.

In exceptional cases an insured who is interested in a loss occurrence can try to feign good intentions prior to conclusion of the insurance contract by means of preventive measures.

Interventions in a risk before and after conclusion of an insurance policy do not therefore always have to be mutually exclusive and can serve in exceptional cases the same purpose. It is extremely difficult for the risk carrier to recognize such exceptional cases in advance. He has to live with them and try to clarify and prove the intentions afterward, after occurrence of the loss.

In general, intervention is effected before conclusion of the policy to risks with no moral hazard, whereas of risks in which intervention following conclusion of the policy provoked losses, it can be said that they were subject to moral hazard. The latter risks would usually not have been accepted by all risk carriers. A positive degree of moral hazard already exists if there is a suspicion that an attempt could be made to influence the risk after conclusion of the policy, and cover of the risk is refused by a risk carrier on the grounds of this suspicion.

4.5.3 *Three Risk Categories*

We want to distinguish between three main categories with the purpose of separating one as the category of risks subject to moral hazard. First, we shall strictly define the categories:

> Category 1: Risk category consisting of "natural risks" in which the occurrence and the amount of losses are independent of the will of any human beings. *Example*: Hurricanes, hail.
>
> Category 2: Risk category consisting of risks which are dependent on human beings, in the occurrence of which, however, no one has an interest. *Example*: Motor third-party liability.
>
> Category 3: Risk category consisting of risks which are dependent on human beings, some of whom may have an interest in the occurrence of a loss event. *Example*: Fidelity insurance, disability insurance.

The risks in category 1 are not subject to moral hazard regardless of whether anyone is interested in their occurrence, as they are not subject to human influence. Risks of category 2 are in principle subject to moral hazard because they can be affected from outside, for example, arson by a pyromaniac; as regards their cover, however, the criterion of moral hazard is of no importance, as a motivation or intention to bring about a loss is missing.

In the case of risks in category 3, it is on the one hand possible to influence the risk and, on the other hand, the intention to bring about a loss cannot be ruled out. In the case of risks of the first two categories, moral hazard can always be ruled out; this is never so in the case of the third category.

This breakdown of risks by category seems acceptable, as the three categories comprise all risks and no risk can belong to two categories at the same time. The three categories are therefore *mutually exclusive risk groups*, which together form a *complete risk system*. Those risks where suspicion of moral hazard exists are separated from all other risks. The concept of moral hazard is directly based on the possibility of affecting the risk and on the intentions of the risk owner or of third parties, and not on the assessment of the risk carrier.

As illuminating as this breakdown of risks by category might appear at first glance, there is a catch: the definitions of the three risk categories are clear and convenient for an analysis, but the allocation of risks to the categories is full of uncertainty and dependent on subjective assessment.

Are hurricanes and hail risks allocatable to category 1 and motor third-party liability risks to category 2 as suggested? The answers to these questions are not unequivocal.

Hurricanes which regularly affect the south and east of the United States can often be located during their development phase in the Caribbean and their future course worked out with a certain probability. By evacuating endangered areas in good time it is possible to reduce the related losses. However, more and more attempts are being made to interfere directly in the development of hurricanes by injecting iodide crystals into the nuclei of the storms in the hope of reducing their energy. Although these experiments promise success, their effects have in no way been scientifically substantiated thus far.

It is a similar state of affairs with experiments with "hail rockets," where by injecting silver iodide crystals it is possible to provoke the outbreak of a rain instead of a hail storm. It is therefore no longer possible to rule out the eventuality that man can affect hurricanes or hail storms even if only to a small extent.

In motor liability we can hope, but in no way be sure, that there are no pathological persons who acquire a car and conclude a liability insurance with the intention of running over another person in a faked accident.

We see that the allocation of risks to the three categories can be quite arbitrary. A critical observer, wanting to take into account even improbable pathological cases, may allocate all or almost all risks to category 3, thus making the allocation of risks to risk categories pointless and preventing us from achieving our goal of *separating* from other risks those risks where the criterion of moral hazard is of importance for the assessment of insurability.

The definitions of categories 1 and 2 should now be changed to such an extent that hurricanes and hail storms and other risks which can be influenced by man only minimally or not at all come into the first category, and motor liability and *almost all risks of the main classes of insurance business* into the second category.

To arrive at a reasonable solution, we shall resort to the conduct of the risk carrier and his assessment of moral hazard. In the *first category* those risks should be explicitly included that can be influenced by human beings very slightly or not at all. The *second* and largest *category* would consist of all those risks with degree of moral hazard zero which are not included in the first category. (The degree of moral hazard was defined in Section 4.5.1.) The *third category* consists of all risks with a positive degree of moral hazard.

The three new categories are again mutually exclusive entities, which together form a complete risk system. The risks subject to moral hazard are clearly separated from those which are not, and the allocation of individual risks to the categories is unequivocal and uncontested. Category 2 contains, as required, almost all risks of the main lines of insurance business (motor, accident, sickness, life, etc.). The concept "degree of moral hazard" has already given us the tool, at least theoretically, to determine the intensity of moral hazard objectively if we know that a risk is in the third risk category.

The question at the end of Section 4.5.1 can now be clearly answered: When clarifying the concept of moral hazard, the criterion should be the conduct of the risk *carriers* and not the motivations and intentions of the risk owners or third parties.

In the following section we shall deal exclusively with risks from the third category.

4.5.4 *Moral Hazard, Interest, Motivation*

In the case of risks with a positive degree of moral hazard, a distinction can be made between various interest groups:

1. The applicant for cover has an interest in a loss occurrence (expects to profit from a loss and is therefore not averse to the occurrence of a loss which he may even provoke).
2. A third party has an interest in a loss occurrence.

In case 1, extreme care should be taken when covering a risk.

In case 2, there may be an additional danger element which has to be taken into account in the premium calculation, even though the applicant for cover is not at fault in any way. The risk carrier should in these circumstances make an effort to seek ways and means to provide the applicant with cover. Such additional danger elements on the part of third parties occur for example in the case of political risks (danger of nationalization).

In surety business the opposite interest situation compared to case 2 appears in a tripartite relationship. The third party is that of a principal who causes the person responsible for the project to take out a surety insurance. The third party is naturally very keen to *prevent* a loss occurrence.

If the applicant for cover is responsible for the fact that a third party would like to do him harm (e.g., because he has provoked the third party), his claim to have cover is greatly weakened. The risk carrier has, as in case 1, to obtain more information and take more care.

Despite this limitation, we can generally say:

Principle 18

> **The degree of insurability of a risk generally decreases to a greater extent if the applicant for cover has an interest in the occurrence of a loss than if third parties show such an interest.**

As already mentioned in Section 4.5.1, we have achieved the transition from the double relation "risk object-risk carrier" to a multiple relation. The more diverse the relation is, the greater the information needed by the risk carrier.

In the case of risks with a positive degree of moral hazard, it often makes no sense to resort to statistical methods since there are no generally reliable laws. It is also dangerous to project into the future experience from the past. Without the help of statistical methods, however, we are groping in the dark with regard to determining the degree of randomness. Nor can we carry out a statistically based rating. Risks with a positive degree of moral hazard, which would be subjectively rejected for that reason, therefore often lie in the conditionally uninsurable area.

From these remarks we can deduce:

Principle 19

> Risks with a positive degree of moral hazard are for the risk carrier often largely unknown, risky, and dangerous. Their degree of insurability is on average *far* below that of risks which are dependent on human beings with degree of moral hazard zero.

The degree of insurability of a risk naturally decreases the more risk carriers refuse it because of uninsurability, and a risk carrier is all the more likely to refuse it, the greater the interest entertained by some party in a loss occurrence.

From this the following can be deduced:

Principle 20

> The degree of insurability of risks with a positive degree of moral hazard decreases *rapidly* with increasing interest of certain parties to bring about a loss and with increasing number of such interested parties.

The insurability decreases rapidly since increasing moral hazard reduces simultaneously the value of other information on the risk and of otherwise relevant statistical material. When borderline cases are examined, where the decision with regard to subjective insurability or uninsurability is not clear from the beginning, the criterion of moral hazard is very often the cause of the indecision.

4.6 Public Policy

4.6.1 *Public Policy and Ethics of Insurance*

First, we should like to recall briefly to the reader the ideals of professional ethics, which in the hard competitive struggle and day-to-day routine often tend to be forgotten.

Whether private or state run, the insurance industry carries out a significant social function and is indeed indispensable in the service sector of the modern world. The management, employees, salespeople, and government officials in the insurance industry should therefore be proud of their profession and be concerned for its reputation. Such pride is all the more important in that the insurance industry is frequently attacked from various quarters and made a scapegoat for all kinds of grievances. One prerequisite for maintaining the industry's reputation is to uphold the *idea of insurance* and *insurance ethics.*

Each professional risk carrier should therefore carefully check whether covering the risks offered him is consistent with public policy; in the long term this is in his own interest as well as that of the industry. The objective quantification of this criterion in our geometric model is carried out in exactly the same way as for moral hazard and is solely dependent on assessment of the risks by the risk carriers.

Public policy is defined in *Black's Law Dictionary* in the following way:

> "... the community common sense and common conscience extended and applied throughout the state to matters of public morals, public health, public

> safety, public welfare, and the like; it is that general and well-settled public opinion relating to man's plain, palpable duty to his fellow men having due regard to all the circumstances of each particular relation and situation."

In the following considerations, in addition to such obvious matters as encouragement of crime, clearly a threat to public welfare, we also regard wastefulness in the economy (e.g., through insurance coverage of trivial risks) to be contrary to public policy.

Public policy considerations are an aspect of insurability which is increasingly coming to the fore. The number of risks in which this question crops up is rapidly growing as a consequence of various socioeconomic and political developments. A few examples are:

1. The growth of urban conglomerations gives rise to friction among the various social classes. This leads to social unrest, bringing with it a host of new risks the cover of which is normally not the task of the insurance industry.
2. The constantly increasing vulnerability of the world of modern technology to organized crime and terrorism is a tempting channel for certain individuals to challenge society. In this respect the insurance industry can only make a limited contribution to stability. We shall revert to this point in Section 4.6.5.
3. The world is closing in. Decisions and resolutions of an economic or financial nature immediately affect more and more people, occur with increasing frequency, have to be taken faster and faster, and compel more and more people to unpleasant actions. More and more situations arise which call for decisions of a far-reaching nature, for which the decision maker has to assume responsibility and

accept the consequences in the event of having been wrong. The resulting, often harsh ways of doing business force more and more enterprises into the corner, inducing them to take speculative risks. *Speculative business risks are not suitable objects for insurance.* That these risks are not suitable for insurance in no way reflects upon the entrepreneur taking the risk. If, for example, a clothing manufacturer decides to devote his entire production for the coming season to the manufacture of blue jeans either because he expects a fashion trend toward blue jeans at that point and hopes to get ahead of his competitors, or because he hopes to avoid excessive competition, he is taking a highly speculative risk and should not be covered by insurance companies against losses which might occur if fashion moves in another direction. This does not, however, say anything about the *character* of the manufacturer.

If speculative risks were covered, the demand for further covers of this nature, which are not compatible with the idea of insurance, would increase, signifying a dangerous and undesirable trend for the insurance industry. Insurance and speculation should remain incompatible concepts.

Principle 21

> The cover of "speculative" entrepreneurial risks is in general not compatible with the idea of insurance.

4.6.2 *Public Policy and the Need for Insurance*

We refer to risks as *trivial* if they can *only* lead to losses which can be borne by the insured without any noticeable burden. Such losses we also call *trivial*. Covering trivial risks should be avoided for two reasons: On the one hand, administrative expenses and loss settlement costs are very high compared with the pure risk premium. The insured must therefore pay a relatively high premium for a cover which in fact he does not need.

On the other hand, this relatively high premium annoys many insureds in the long run and prompts them to try to get back the money spent by notifying losses which never in fact occurred. *Covering trivial risks can therefore act as an incentive to dishonesty.*

Expenses incurred in processing and investigating trivial losses have to be passed on to the insureds, who may be expected to complain about the risk carrier's high premiums and pettiness in claim settlement. If the losses are, however, not investigated but simply paid without further ado, word soon gets around about such generosity, and this creates a further incentive for dishonesty. The vicious circle is closed. No matter how the risk carrier acts, he will annoy many an insured and/or provoke dishonesty.

For years we have observed in many countries losses on the part of the insurance industry in, for example, covering theft (not robbery or burglary) of personal belongings. In some markets such covers are not granted any more or are only given under very restricted conditions. Coverage of trivial risks has also contributed to worsening the image of the insurance industry.

Principle 22

> Covering risks for which no real need for insurance exists is inconsistent with public policy and should in principle be avoided.

Three ways can be envisaged of avoiding this problem:

1. Covers, against theft for example, can be added to other covers. The applicant should only be able to obtain such a

cover in conjunction with another more comprehensive one. This solution would shift onto more profitable lines of business the relatively high costs of a less profitable one and in this way achieve a balanced result on a broader basis. As we shall see in Section 4.6.4, such a procedure is unsound, since every line of insurance business should be self-supporting in the long run. The problems arising from coverage of trivial losses are therefore mitigated somewhat in this solution, but are in no way eliminated.

2. The professional risk carrier can refuse to cover risks in certain lines of business. This attitude is not ideal either and is also difficult to maintain, although we prefer it to the first solution.

In Section 4.4.3, when the utility function was introduced, we saw that a person will assess the value of a certain amount of money according to his character and financial circumstances. He will therefore also subjectively decide what losses can be borne and where the limit of his personal insurance needs lies.

By refusing to cover all risks of a certain line of business (of small risks), the risk carrier will also have to decline applicants for whom the cover of certain small risks in fact corresponds to a personal need if not an absolute necessity. This would not enhance his reputation among the public. In addition, he is running the risk of losing certain customers to competitors who, according to solution 1, offer comprehensive covers including the cover in question.

3. We envisage the following as the best solution: The risk carrier offers comprehensive covers which provide for a minimal deductible and offers as alternatives other, higher deductibles. Naturally, as the deductible increases, the premium must fall. The minimum deductible should be fixed in such a way that it can be borne by each insured without difficulty.

What does the risk carrier achieve by offering such a product?

1. He eliminates all *objectively trivial losses* which would not be a genuine burden to the insured. In so

doing he diverts himself of the problems which arise in connection with such losses.

2. He relieves himself not only of trivial losses from "trivial lines," but also from other lines of business, enabling him to greatly reduce administrative and loss-settlement expenses.
3. By grading the deductibles he can assume an important advisory function and adapt the cover to the individual needs of the applicant. He therefore eliminates not only objectively trivial but also *subjectively trivial losses* from the cover and has a good chance of satisfying the customer.

Principle 23

> Trivial losses unsuitable for insurance can best be eliminated by offering comprehensive covers with a range of deductibles.

Remark

In Principle 7 we stated that a risk is generally (i.e., not always) the more insurable the smaller the average loss upon occurrence. This qualification was made with an eye upon trivial losses, for which the principle does not hold. Principle 7 is valid as long as the average claim is not too small. For trivial losses criteria b (maximum possible loss) and c (average claim amount) are fully satisfied, but not, however, criterion g (public policy).

4.6.3 *How Risks Consistent with Public Policy Can Cease to Be So as a Consequence of an Insurance Cover*

Insurance companies and professional risk carriers in general are for many people anonymous powers hidden away in luxurious office buildings. It is easy for the man in the street to acquire a negative image of the insurance industry, and not so easy for the industry to supplant this with a more positive one. The average person often feels at such a disadvantage when dealing with an insurance company that he is not prepared to act with the same fairness used in his normal everyday business dealings. The view is widely held that cheating an insurance company does no real harm to anyone. Even persons who would shrink from an outright insurance fraud think nothing of submitting slightly exaggerated bills for medical expenses or repairs or replacement of damaged property—if they now that there is insurance. Presenting inflated bills for services rendered, which one would not do in respect of an *uninsured* patient or customer, seems quite natural when an *insurer* is in the background to foot the bill. The voice of conscience is silent vis-à-vis the anonymous risk carrier.

At the same time the injured party finds no reason to challenge the excessive charges, since he has faithfully paid his insurance premiums and now it is the turn of the risk carrier to meet *his* obligations. There is no obvious reason why he should defend the interests of his insurer. He finds it quite natural that he was first asked if he was insured or not before the price was determined.

The danger of the state of affairs described is that it is not recognized as being incorrect. It is therefore difficult to combat this way of thinking.

It is inequitable to keep two price categories for the same services and to use one or the other depending on whether the customer is insured or not. By covering certain risks, the risk carrier can unintentionally push up the amounts claimed in the event of loss; this certainly contradicts the principle of insurance, according to which insurance cover should indemnify the policyholder in the event of a loss but not, however, serve to enrich him—or, as in the case described previously, a third party. Here we come up against the paradoxical situation where, *as a consequence of taking out an insurance cover, a risk suitable for insurance might become unsuitable.*

The practice of tolerating excessive claims by third parties conceals grave dangers. No less dangerous, albeit considered with less tolerance, are generous agreements between the insureds and the third parties concerned at the expense of the risk carrier. Here the insured bears a direct responsibility for the excessive prices demanded.

The increased prices have to be passed on to the insureds after a time lag in the form of premium increases, which can lead to general discontent and be detrimental to the reputation of the insurance industry. The risk carriers are not the cause but rather co-sufferers in this malaise. Particularly in the liability and accident lines, a cost pressure is felt upon the unsettled losses of previous years, and the original tariffs and reserve amounts often prove subsequently to have been too low. The risk carrier can remain in a loss position for a long time either because he recognized too late or has underestimated a price increase or because he only received permission to increase premiums with some delay.

The situation becomes particularly critical when the additional costs have to be passed on to a relatively small group of insureds, and the premiums for the individual soar to such an extent that he may be unable to afford a badly needed cover. Such a situation has arisen in the United States in medical malpractice insurance.

How can the insurance industry prevent the situation where, by taking out a policy, risks which are suitable for insurance become unsuitable with all the resultant hazards and consequences?

We have already mentioned that an *incorrect act* which is not generally recognized by society as such is particularly difficult to deal with. The fight has to be carried out on several fronts.

1. An educational campaign is necessary to make clear to insureds that excessive claims will in the long run have repercussions in the form of higher premiums. If the insured finds the prices demanded too high as compared with the service he receives, he should protest in his own interest or inform his insurance company.

2. In certain lines of business the fact that there is insurance cover demonstrably leads to the submission of unjustified and excessive claims. In respect of automobile material

damage the risk carrier now has the possibility to counteract this trend by means of better documentation, giving exact quantification of the amount of damage instead of mere estimates and at less expense than with the estimates used earlier.

3. In certain lines of business (e.g., in motor collision), a standard list of the usual market costs of repairs and spare parts can be compiled and a list made of firms which undertake to adhere to the price list. The insured can be obliged in the event of a loss to seek one of these listed firms if he wants to benefit from a reduced standard premium adjusted to the respective prices. If he does not want to adhere to the list, he should not benefit from the reduced premium.

Although the procedure just described has by no means been realized in practice, certain risk carriers in motor collision business already take into account in their rating the differential repair and spare parts costs by *make* of car as determined *on the basis of experiment in their own workshops.*

4. If amounts are claimed under insurance policies which exceed his tolerance limits, the risk carrier should not shy away from legal action.

5. The most effective means of combatting excessive prices would presumably be for the insured to be required to retain a sufficiently large share of the risk so that it is in *his* immediate interest to resist outrageous prices.

Using such measures as these, the risk carrier can wage an effective fight against dishonesty in insurance and prevent risks suitable for insurance, the cover of which the individual often urgently needs, from becoming unsuitable for insurance. In addition, he can make a contribution to fighting inflation, increase his subjective area of insurability, and, finally, as we have seen, render his insureds and the insurance industry a real service.

4.6.4 *Public Policy and Collective Fairness*

In the last section we mentioned the critical situation which arises when a risk carrier has to pass on to a relatively small group of insureds the additional expenditure caused by payment of excessive claims. Would it not be more acceptable to spread these additional costs over a greater area, that is, also to insureds in lines of business in which excessive payments do not or hardly ever occur? In Section 4.6.2 it was mentioned that the relatively high costs associated with certain troublesome losses of a trivial nature could be passed on to another line of business with better results.

The list of reasons given in the last two sections that may make certain lines of business chronically unprofitable can be extended even further. Just as long, however, is the list of instances in which the deficits of chronically bad lines of business are borne by healthy ones. Here examples would be industrial fire business "financed" in many countries by the good results of household insurance; burglary business, which in many cases can be transacted at inadequate terms thanks to the good results of simple fire business; or medical malpractice insurance in Germany, which has been underrated for some time because risk carriers hope to offset this by other covers on the usually well-off medical profession.

According to the idea of insurance, all possible insurance covers should be broken down geographically, by line of business, and within each line in such a way that homogeneous groups of similar risks are established. Within these groups a balance in time and in numbers should be sought.

Example: In life insurance we have a breakdown into homogeneous groups by age and health status.

If the premiums within one group become too high for the individuals in that group, the risk carrier has to take certain measures, such as for example those recommended in the last section. Under no circumstances, however, should he raise the premiums of other groups, since in this case he would be going against the basic idea of insurance. Each homogeneous group of insureds should be *self-supporting*, that is, able to finance over the long run the losses incurred by the group through payment of appropriate premiums.

The insureds in a sound, self-supporting, homogeneous group should not have to make extra payments in the form of premium increases to help support the covers of an ailing line of business which in no way brings them any advantage or additional security. Each insured should be expected to pay a premium for the cover he himself needs and for that cover only.

By trying to spread losses over the various more or less independent homogeneous groups of insureds, the risk carrier overrates some risks and underrates others, therefore infringing upon the principle of collective fairness. In doing this he is pursuing a short-sighted business policy, since he drives away the insureds in the overrated, healthy lines of business and attracts applicants for cover of underrated risks. *He therefore not only acts unfairly but engages in a dangerous antiselection against himself.*

When a group is no longer self-supporting and cannot be restored to health by appropriate measures, it is more reasonable and the lesser evil to get rid of the risks in question, since they have entered the subjective area of uninsurability.

Principle 24

> A risk carrier should avoid, wherever possible, passing the high costs of one line of business onto another.

4.6.5 *Public Policy and the Fighting of Crime, Terrorism, and Social Unrest*

External factors such as the rapid growth of social unrest, crime, or terrorism can transform risks suitable for insurance into unsuitable ones. This may appear unjust, since the private individual might under certain circumstances which he himself has not caused to occur no longer find cover for formerly insurable risks. The individual might be deprived of cover precisely when the need for it is greater than before. The professional risk carrier therefore has the duty to look for suitable measures for shifting the risks in question into the area of insurability and help the individual meet his cover needs.

The above-mentioned external factors can make endangered risks uncalculable and push them along the premium axis outside the area of insurability. In the case of threats such as destruction of property, the risks affected can cease to be of a random nature and be shifted along the axis of degree of randomness outside the area of insurablity.

Above all, however, the external factors mentioned can go beyond the limits of the insurance industry's proper sphere of activity. Covering risks prone to crime or terrorism not only often makes no sense; it can, as we shall see, even turn out to be dangerous as long as the responsible national and international bodies do not attack the causes of terrorism and social unrest at the roots. Coverages of this sort are in many cases clearly contrary to public policy.

How can an insurance cover act as an additional incentive for terrorists and criminals? The underlying idea has already been described in Section 4.6.3, but we shall now explain it using the example of *ransom demand following kidnapping*. Recent events have shown that demands for ransom can arise from both purely criminal and politically motivated kidnapping. Consequently, major companies are increasingly seeking kidnapping insurance for their executives, especially in countries where kidnapping is a particularly grave hazard. It is obvious that the existence of such a cover, if known, serves as a special incentive to criminals and terrorists who might believe that they can make their demands even more exorbitant and have them met more easily. Also, the number of people "worth kidnapping" is increased by the issue of insurance cover on such risks. Experience has unfortunately shown that the only promising way of fighting terrorism is to show firmness, no matter how inhuman this might appear in a particular case of kidnapping, since each terrorist action which achieves its goal only provokes further such deeds.

Inciting people to crime on the part of the risk carrier must be avoided at all costs and is inconsistent with public policy.

Risk carriers can take the following measures to live up to their obligations toward society in general and to their insureds in particular:

1. By means of special clauses, the insured should be motivated to safeguard the interests of the risk carrier. This includes, for example, a silence clause which obliges the insured, in the event of a kidnapping, not to comment on or even to deny the existence of a ransom insurance cover.

   In the event of cover against property damage during a riot, the insured should be obliged to take strict security measures (locks, alarms, etc.). We are, however, of the opinion that such risks are already at the limit of objective uninsurability for the private insurance industry, since is would seem the proper function of the state to protect the citizen and his property in the event of a riot and to indemnify any related losses.
2. The insured should retain a share of the risk, in the form of a percentage share or a flat deductible, and/or have realistic cover limits appropriate to his security needs. (It is no coincidence that we have already encountered such measures in Section 4.6.2 and 4.6.3.) He should also be rewarded with a premium bonus in the event of special safety measures.
3. The risk carrier should maintain contacts with the security forces of the state and seek advice on the behavior to pursue in concrete cases of kidnapping and the like.

Since the private insurance industry has responsibilities toward society, it should seek contact with the appropriate government bodies and support them as far as possible in their fight against the causes of social unrest, terrorism, and crime. This can be most effectively done by means of an association in which all insurance companies are represented, which acts on behalf of the entire insurance industry and which can make binding commitments.

Such a policy would not only do a service to society but also serve the private insurance industry's own interests, since it would combat a development which renders more and more risks more dangerous or even uninsurable and more and more frequently puts the risk carrier in the embarrassing position of having to refuse cover for risks precisely when the applicant for cover most urgently needs it.

We conclude:

Principle 25

> Risks suitable for insurance can become unsuitable because of external circumstances (crime, terrorism, social unrest). This development should be fought in conjunction with the insureds and the responsible government bodies.

Remark

If otherwise normal risks are subject to the additional risk of being nationalized, we consider them to be less unsuitable for insurance than risks which are subject to terrorism and civil commotion, since in the event of nationalization without compensation the insured cannot count on the aid of any government body. The state itself is then the factor which causes loss of property. Only a private insurance company could be a possible risk carrier here. Nevertheless, for other reasons, nationalization risks often lie in the dark gray zone or in the area of uninsurability.

4.7 Legal Restrictions

4.7.1 *Legal Restrictions: An "Objective" Insurability Criterion*

From Section 3.2 we know that the insurability criterion *legal restrictions* can only assume two values in the geometric model, the value 0 when the risk can be covered within existing legal restrictions and the value 1 when this is not so.

Whether a risk is insurable in terms of legal restrictions does not depend on the characteristics of the individual, private professional risk carrier and on his assessment of the risk but on the legislator. This criterion of insurability is distinguished therefore in one essential point from all previously discussed insurability criteria:

Principle 26

> The insurability criterion *legal restrictions* is basically an objective criterion independent of any subjective assessment.

Here a minor reservation should be made in that difficulties in interpretation of the law might occur in borderline cases, although as soon as a legal decision has been made and a precedent established, the objectivity in the assessment of insurability is again restored.

A further objection might be that one risk carrier sees possibilities of covering a risk by getting round legal restrictions, whereas another does not recognize such possibilities. For the first insurer the risk would be subjectively insurable, for the second, not. In this special case, we would have a displacement of the insurability criterion *legal restrictions* onto the subjective level. This displacement, which could only arise from not knowing each and every actual possibility within the framework set up by the legislator, would necessitate the creation of a gray zone on the h-axis (legal restrictions), corresponding somewhat to those on the f-axis (moral hazard) and the g-axis (public policy).

Here again we encounter, as in Section 4.4.2, the fact that lack of information greatly affects the subjective insurability of risks. Whereas earlier it was only a case of immediate information about the risk itself, the information now affects legal restrictions which do not lie directly in the nature of the risk.

Scanty information can also, by the way, lead to the risk carrier's not only declining legally permissible risks but also granting legally prohibited covers. We can take it, however, that practically every professional risk carrier has a competent legal advisor, and that confusion of this sort does not arise in practice. Principle 26 thus regains its validity, and the risks can only assume the values 0 and 1 on the h-axis (no gray zone).

4.7.2 Legal Restrictions Determined a Posteriori

We can distinguish between three kinds of legal restrictions; they will be discussed in this and the next two sections. First, there are legal restrictions that do not refer to risks but to deeds and actions. These restrictions are set down in *insurance contract law* and will be discussed in this section, whereas the limits dealt with in the next two sections have to do with regulation by the *supervisory authorities*.

In Sections 4.5 and 4.6 we have dealt with risks involving possible misuse of insurance covers. It is the task of the risk carrier to decide whether he wants to accept or reject such risks because of moral hazard or public policy considerations.

The law now prescribes in many countries that a cover be invalidated upon occurrence of the loss *if the loss is deliberately caused by the insured.* In many countries, cover is even invalidated by *gross negligence*. Such laws extend to all risks where the insured has the possibility of affecting the occurrence of a loss.

The law is not applied to risks where misuse of insurance cover is to be feared, but only where *such misuse actually takes place*.

If a loss has been caused intentionally, we can say *after the fact* that this insured risk was not insurable: from the point of view of the law, the conclusion is drawn after the fact and the loss amount claimed is not paid by the insurer. The loss burden has to be borne by the causer of the loss. *A posteriori*, it can be said that the insurer need not have exercised his function as risk carrier.

Remark

We have already presented some a posteriori considerations in Section 4.5.2 in respect of risks intentionally affected after conclusion of the policy. A posteriori considerations might also occur in the case of the insurability criterion *insurance premium*, and they are particularly important in the field of reinsurance. A posteriori premiums are premiums which depend on the loss experience and which are often only settled finally when the loss is definitely known. Premiums which provide for a profit commission for the reinsured in the event of favorable loss experience and sliding scale premiums are familiar examples of a posteriori reinsurance premiums. Later premium adjustments can serve to bring risks within the combined insurability areas of insurer and reinsurer.

4.7.3 *Cover Prohibitions for Private Insurance*

Let us now split up all risk carriers into private risk carriers and nonmonopolistic state risk carriers in competition with them on the one hand and monopolistic state risk carriers on the other hand. Various reasons (e.g., lack of capacity on the part of the private insurance industry) may cause legislators to nationalize certain branches of the insurance industry and to put them under a state-run monopoly. The weight attached to the reasons varies from country to country to a considerable extent and leads also to the fact that the branches of insurance taken over by the state are very different in the various countries where such government action has occurred.

Here *certain branches of insurance are declared uninsurable by law for private risk carriers* or the latter may merely be allowed to grant certain supplementary covers. Under objective insurability of risks we only want to take into account private risk carriers and their nonmonopolistic state competitors. Then, by definition, the risks in all categories which by law the private insurance industry is not permitted to insure are not insurable. Such risks assume the value 1 on the h-axis.

If we were to incorporate the monopolistic state risk carriers into our observations, the risks falling within the nationalized branches of insurance would be "almost uninsurable." They could in fact be covered by no insurer with the exception of one. (If the monopolistic state carrier goes under more than one name, we still regard him as one carrier.) Is it then reasonable to label risks as uninsurable or almost uninsurable when under certain circumstances there even exists compulsory insurance coverage of them, that is, when the state apparently defines them to be insurable?

An *example* will illustrate that this question cannot be answered easily: Let us examine compulsory social security with the state being the monopolistic risk carrier. Social insurance benefits are not cheap, and they are particularly difficult to maintain when the tax screw cannot be tightened any further and the state cannot summon up any additionally needed sources of income. Moreover, in most industrialized, socially progressive countries there is likely to be a fall in the population over the next few decades and at the same time a reduction of the percentage of the working population in the total population. "Overaging" will increase. The burden on the working section of the population, which finances social insurance benefits, will increase until it reaches a saturation point. As most national budgets are already in the red today, there can be no serious thought of setting aside adequate reserves now to guarantee continuation of social insurance benefits in the future. The consequence is that the state often resorts to the *"pay-as-you-go" system*. Social security contributions are not put aside for the future benefit of the contributers (*level premium system*) but are immediately distributed among the current recipients of benefits. In fact, nowadays most, if not all, social security schemes are already operating on the pay-as-you-go system.

There are naturally great dangers implicit in such a system: If as a result of recession or rise in the ratio of old people in the population, a saturation point is reached and not enough money flows into the coffers of the social security system, the state, in the absence of reserves to fall back on, will be compelled to cut back on social insurance benefits. It will *have to reduce pension payments*, possibly *increase retirement age*, or take other undesirable measures.

An insurance company cannot and must not fail to meet its financial obligations to its insureds. Therefore, it cannot base its business policy on the pay-as-you-go system; the legislator, in the interest of the public, wisely prohibits such a business policy for the private insurance industry, although the state practices it itself in its capacity as social insurer.

Here we come across the interesting phenomenon that the state as champion of social progress and protector of its citizens subjects itself as a risk carrier to far fewer restrictions than the private risk carriers under its control.

The question naturally arises in this context as to whether the state as risk carrier should not have to adhere to the strict rules of its own insurance supervisory authorities. Such a policy would mean a slowing down of social progress somewhat, but would, however, result in better guarantees to the citizen that promises of benefits would be kept in real terms. There are of course numerous pros and cons involved here, which will not be dealt with further.

The question also arises as to whether an institution operating on the pay-as-you-go system can properly be regarded as a risk carrier and, moreover, whether the designation "social security" is not misleading.

Finally, there is the following question: Does the pay-as-you-go system contradict the idea of insurance? We are of the opinion that it does, since *a given group of insureds does not cover itself* with its premium contributions *but rather another group altogether* and, when it later needs cover itself, is dependent upon the contributions of yet other groups. It is doubtful whether a group actually receives in full the benefits equivalent in real terms to its own contributions.

If we now revert to our original question as to whether risks for which there is compulsory insurance can be "almost uninsurable," we cannot exclude a positive answer. In respect of the preceding example, we should question the justification of the expression "compulsory insurance" and replace it by an expression such as "compulsory contribution for social benefits."

We now see more closely why we wanted to exclude monopolistic, state risk carriers from our comments, since they are subject to insurability standards different from those of other risk carriers. A risk insured according to the pay-as-you-go system is not necessarily insurable according to the level premium system.

If a branch of insurance is nationalized in one country and not in a second, we can investigate risks from this branch of insurance as to their insurability in the second country and thereby include them in our insurability considerations. We therefore only have to exclude examination of risks as to their insurability in branches of insurance which are nationalized everywhere.

4.7.4 *Restrictions on the Individual Risk Carrier*

In the last section we pointed out that the state, which has to safeguard the interests of the citizen, subjects the private risk carrier to restrictions on covers which may be granted. Another category of restrictions consists of all manner of regulations designed to protect the financial soundness of the private risk carrier in order to guarantee that he is able to fulfill his obligations toward the insureds. Thus, for example, the state may prescribe solvency margins or issue investment policy guidelines.

In contrast to the limits set a posteriori and the covers prohibited for the private insurance industry as a whole, such regulations as solvency margin requirements are related neither to the policyholder nor to the risk, but to the individual risk carrier. If a potential or actual risk carrier cannot or will not adhere to the regulations, he is either not granted a license to insure risks or he is deprived of an existing one. Subjectively, all risks are then uninsurable for him. He can be excluded from the circle of risk carriers and from the scope of our considerations.

4.7.5 *Legal Cover Provisions*

Legal cover provisions are often encountered in branches where there is compulsory cover. Compulsory cover is enforced by the state so that it can meet its liabilities as protector of the citizen.

A legislator wishing to protect persons injured through no fault of their own in traffic accidents may, for example, make motor liability insurance compulsory, likely with a specified minimum cover legally provided for. Having decreed that every motor car owner must conclude a third-party liability policy, the legislator also has a moral obligation to see that cover is available at a fair premium. He therefore not only prescribes minimum cover, but also exerts an influence on the premium rating in many countries.

Liability is a long-term line of business which is particularly exposed to inflation. A delay in granting permission to effect a necessary premium increase in motor third-party liability can have catastrophic effects on certain risk carriers and, for them, force all the risks belonging to this line of business into the area of uninsurability.

Also in the interests of the insured, the legislator must take into consideration the interests of the risk carrier and maintain the prescribed rates at a fair level not only for the insured but also for the insurer. It is in fact important that the risk carrier constantly keep the legislator aware of his obligations as described and help him fulfill them.

In addition to delayed permission for a necessary premium increase, the motor third-party liability insurer can be hard hit by the tendency observed in some countries for the legislator to give an ever wider interpretation to his duty to protect third parties. *Strict liability*, which in recent times has permeated legal practice in more and more countries, corresponds, for example, to a broader interpretation of the *protective role of government* than does *negligence liability*.

As each risk carrier is free to decide whether he wants to accept the legal cover restrictions or to renounce any activity in the particular line of business affected, the question arises once more as to the validity of Principle 26. Is it possible to maintain under these circumstances that the insurability criterion of legal restrictions is an objective criterion independent of subjective assessment?

We are of the opinion that this is so, since if a risk carrier complies with the legal provisions and nevertheless rejects certain risks (provided that this is legally permissible in the first place), then he refuses to cover certain risks because other criteria are not satisfied; the criterion of legal restrictions is however satisfied. If, on the other hand, a risk carrier does not comply with the legal provisions, he cannot operate in the line of business concerned and does not belong to the body of all professional risk carriers considered in our remarks in respect of that line.

4.7.6 *The Reasons for Legal Restrictions*

In the last four sections we were able to distinguish between four different types of legal restrictions and regulations. They derive from various causes and pursue various goals.

If we disregard political or even opportunist motives, it is possible to pick out a common basis for all restrictions and regulations: the duty of the state to look after the well-being of its citizens and its endeavors to live up to this obligation. Linked with this common basis is the principle, embodied also in the insurance contract law, that the weaker party has to be legally protected.

Let us now list two goals or obligations of the state which might prompt it to make private risk carriers subject to certain regulations.

1. *Upholding the idea of insurance:* Upholding the idea of insurance, in particular the principle of fairness, falls partly within the duty of the state. We have already mentioned losses caused by intentional acts. Such acts contradict the idea of insurance, and the insured's right to receive compensation from the risk carrier is voided by the law in such cases. Through such laws the legislator protects the risk carrier against abuse, but also society: on the one hand, a contribution is made to combatting crime and, on the other, it is prevented that the costs of intentionally caused losses be passed on to the community of insureds in the form of premium increases.

We have seen that the state itself grants covers on the pay-as-you-go system; it is at least doubtful that this system is compatible with the idea of insurance. Here, however, the idea of insurance must give way to another major obligation of the state.

2. *Obligation of the state to guarantee the protection of its citizens where possible:* The citizen has a *right to protection.* This protection may be compulsory, as with social security, for example, regardless of whether the individual citizen considers it to be necessary or not; it can also be in the form of provisions for private risk carriers to guarantee where possible that policyholders always pay a fair premium and, in the event of loss, actually receive the insurance benefits due. Such provisions are very strict and particularly important in life insurance. Regulation in the liability branch was referred to in the last section. With regard to protection of the citizen against civil commotion, see Example 7 in Chapter 6.

4.8 Cover Limits

In Section 3.1 we mentioned that the cover limits criterion was the only one of the nine insurability criteria that could not be given a numerical representation. The sum of all cover limits corresponds to an enormous amorphous mass of clauses, regulations, restrictions, and the like, which cannot be globally and quantitatively expressed in a reasonable way, but can only be broken down by line of business, type of treaty, or other characteristics.

In general, we can identify two intentions which a risk carrier pursues when establishing cover limits:

1. He seeks to achieve a certain protection, which he deems necessary, against abuse, against violation of the principle of property and liability insurance, that indemnities paid should not be greater than losses suffered, against a high frequency of trivial losses, and so on.
2. At the same time the risk carrier tries to alter the risks in such a way that, on the one hand, they fall within the insurability area and, on the other, the related cover still seems worthwhile to the applicant.

Here we are naturally speaking of risks which would be uninsurable for the risk carrier *without* cover limits.

Some important and frequently occurring cover limits refer immediately to the insurability criteria *maximum possible loss* and *moral hazard*. Many risks are subjectively only insurable in terms of these two criteria once cover limits have been established.

In Section 4.7.4 we mentioned legal restrictions such as prescribed minimum solvency margins or investment policy guidelines concerning the individual risk carrier, designed to protect him against insolvency or even ruin for the benefit of citizens insured with him. The risk carrier establishes cover limits in the interest of his own continued existence. Legal restrictions and cover limits have the same goal—to protect the risk carrier against ruin—although the motives are different. It is therefore understandable that they often complement each other well as flanking safeguards.

At various points we have already drawn attention to the need to establish certain cover limits, for example when considering cover for crime, terrorism, and social unrest in Section 4.6.5, when outlining measures aimed at preventing risks suitable for insurance from becoming unsuitable as a consequence of cover (Section 4.6.3), when stressing the advantages of introducing cover limits in the form of deductibles in certain cases (e.g., in Sections 4.4.2 and 4.6.2), and so on.

It would be difficult to keep a discussion of clauses and treaty conditions, broken down by line of business, treaty types, and the like, on an easily understandable level, and such a discussion would go beyond the scope of this study in any event. We shall therefore devote our attention to just one more interesting special problem.

The cover limits which a reinsurer seeks are often of quite another type than those of the direct insurer. The *shifting of priorities* in respect of cover limits when going from direct insurance to reinsurance is to a high degree characteristic of the reinsurance business and would be worthy of a separate study. In reinsurance we are familiar with various types of treaties, which are more or less appropriate for the different lines of business, countries, and portfolios. The different types of reinsurance cover are characteristic of certain types of cover limits. The individual cover limits result from the individual treaty provisions.

Example

For a "limited excess of loss reinsurance," the upper and lower limits of the covered layer are the characteristic cover limits. Within these limits the cover is 100%. In the excess of loss cover in the liability line we come up against the following shift of priorities:

Large losses are as a rule only settled after several years. By the time they are finally settled, many losses which were originally below the deductible of the direct insurer (lower limit) come within the layer as a consequence of inflation. The reinsurer experiences *inflation in the number of losses*. The average loss in the layer above the lower cover limit is also affected by a certain inflation, the *inflation in the excess loss amount,* the level of which depends on the lower and upper limits. The inflation factors in the number and amount of losses have a multiplicative effect. In many countries it has been observed that large losses are exposed to a growing readiness on the part of law courts to make high awards and/or are exposed to a greatly increasing pressure on medical costs. They are therefore subject not only to the usual claims inflation but also to a *superimposed inflation,* which burdens the reinsured layer.

These inflation effects lead to an inflation explosion for the excess of loss reinsurer, against which he has to protect himself in some way. His inflation is a multiple of the claims inflation to which the direct insurer is exposed.

Here we recognize a clear shift of priorities in respect of cover limits. Because of the nature of the excess of loss cover, it becomes a prime task for the reinsurer to protect himself against rampant inflation. This protection is often achieved by means of the "stability" or "index" clause, which provides for the lower layer limit and often also the upper layer limit to increase with an inflation index (e.g., wage index) and divides up in this way the additional inflation burden between direct insurer and reinsurer.

The risk carrier must naturally take into account the safety needs of the reinsurer and the just-mentioned shift of priorities when meeting these needs. It affects his insurability area and thereby also indirectly his premium and acceptance policy. The reinsurance therefore draws attention to phenomena which a risk carrier could easily have overlooked to his own disadvantage had he not taken out a reinsurance cover.

Insurability Limits and the Policyholder

Like a professional risk carrier, each person also has his own individual insurability area, demarcated by a boundary line from the individual area of uninsurability. "Person" is taken here to mean a real or corporate person. Similarly, as with professional risk carriers, we can also define and examine objective areas of insurability and uninsurability for groups of persons. Such an examination does not, however, lead us very far in our analysis of the insurability of risks—the goal of this study. Why?

By the nature of the matter, we are interested in risks in the gray zone, on the edges of the insurability and uninsurability areas. Risks for which no insurance cover is sought, since they can *easily* be borne by the individual are subjectively—usually also objectively—insurable. Risks of this type are particularly numerous and difficult to express, since they do not appear in the world of insurance business. They can usually be included in the objective area of insurance as defined in Chapter 2 or can be excluded from the considerations of insurability without any noticeable impact. We shall therefore exclude this group of risks from our considerations because of the difficulty in expressing them.

Another, much smaller group comprises those risks for which individuals seek no insurance cover, although they themselves are aware that they *cannot easily* bear the risks, *knowing from the start that the risks are uninsurable*, because they do not satisfy certain insurability criteria. In accordance with Principle 21, many speculative entrepreneurial risks fall in this category. Such risks usually belong to the objective area of uninsurability defined in Chapter 2 and are difficult to express, because they too are not encountered in the insurance world. We shall likewise exclude these from our considerations.

In a third category we can summarize all risks for which an "external" cover is sought. This is the only category that interests us and the one we have examined in this study. Since professional risk carriers have to be consulted when covers are requested, their risk assessment is decisive for the determination of insurability. *We have therefore concentrated our considerations, and rightly so, on professional risk carriers.* Instead of persons, we frequently referred to applicants for cover.

We have always included applicants for cover in our considerations when their attitude and actual or possible conduct had a bearing on the criteria of insurability of professional risk carriers or were even of decisive significance for the insurability of risks in the view of the risk carriers. References to the applicants for cover can be found for example in Section 4.4.3 when considering the risk premium and utility theory, or in Sections 4.5 (moral hazard) and 4.6 (public policy). In Section 4.7 we included in our deliberations the legislator, who prescribes certain relations between persons and risk carriers (e.g., compulsory covers) and is committed to the protection of the applicant, by which he affects the insurability of certain risks.

At various points we tried to probe the means (e.g., cover limits, reinsurance cover) and guidelines which an insurer's business policy should adopt so as to grant the cover required wherever possible, or if this cannot be achieved, to provide for a reasonable alternative.

We have eliminated from our considerations direct relations between person and risk. In this way we have avoided unnecessary digression without having omitted any essential aspect of the evaluation of insurability. At the same time, however, we have also avoided unwelcome complications.

Remark 1

If we were to refer the insurability of risks primarily to private and corporate persons, we would have to change or extend the definitions established in Chapter 2. A possible definition of subjective insurability would be: If a *risk* related to a *person* could theoretically be insured by at least one *risk carrier*, regardless of whether such a cover is sought or not, then this risk is insurable. In such a case, we objectify the definition, as we place the whole of the gray zone in the insurability area and leave it open whether the person actually seeks a cover or not. The definition is reasonable since the person who seeks a cover at certain terms also receives it, if it is obtainable at all from some risk carrier or other, provided he looks around long enough. Since finding a cover as a rule depends on the risk and the conditions and less on the person seeking it, the definition is objective rather than subjective.

As a consequence of the preceding definition of insurability, the gray zone is dropped and quite an essential element in the analysis of insurability is lost. Although we have now included in our definition of insurability the three levels person, risk carrier, and risk, instead of the previous two (risk carrier, risk), we have suffered a major loss of information. Here we see one reason why insurability investigations should be concentrated on professional risk carriers and risks alone.

Remark 2

A further reason why insurability investigations should refer to the risk carrier rather than to the applicant for cover is the following: A risk carrier must decide whether or not he wants to *assume* the cover of a risk, whereas the individual person seeks to *pass on* the risk. The insurability of the risk is decided by the issue of the cover and not by the search for it. Since there are no restriction on the mere search for cover, *irrespective of the risk concerned,* no reasonable insurability criteria can be established based on this factor. Such criteria would have to distinguish between risks for which cover can be sought and those for which cover cannot be sought.

Remark 3

We should now like to point out a possible semantic fallacy: A person could be described as "self-insurer" of the risks not actually ceded by him to some risk carrier. From such a terminology, it would follow that *any arbitrary* risk would be insurable either by professional risk carriers or "self-insurers." This would mean that the circle of risk carriers, extended to include private and corporate persons (and state institutions), would have an area of insurability containing all risks, including those rejected by all professional risk carriers, as well as those never even offered for cover because it was clear from the start that they would not be accepted. This would not only contradict all our former remarks, but would make examination of the insurability of risks superfluous. Where is the fallacy?

It is not accurate to say that the private or corporate person functions as "self-insurer" in respect of uninsured risks. Characteristic of insurance cover is replacement in case of a loss, but replacement is not characteristic of "self-insurance." *The uninsured risk is not "self-insured"* but *is borne* by the private or corporate person, whereby it is often doubtful in the event of a loss if the burden can be carried. If losses from uninsured risks can be borne without difficulty by the person, these risks can be included in the area of individual insurability.

Remark 4

A person acquiring an object of value for which cover is an absolute necessity must be aware that insurance premiums belong to the "maintenance costs" of the object. He is imposing on himself a risk which it costs money to cover. If the money for this is not available, then it would not be advisable to buy the object in the first place. We can also say that the object of value is outside the subjective limits of insurability of the individual and that the money available for the required cover is not sufficient to bring the object within the area of insurability of the risk carrier, which is why purchase of the object is not advisable.

Remark 5

A small philosophical reflection: In the field of modern quantum mechanics, *all natural occurrences* are regarded as being random (i.e., events which cannot be exactly predicted). This natural indeterminism is closely linked with the concept of risk. The "smallest possible degree of randomness" is described by Heisenberg's uncertainty principle.

In connection with these remarks it can be deduced in quantum mechanics that an experimenter can never fully exclude himself from the experiment. He cannot watch it from outside. He is part of the experiment.

Now all risks can be thought of as experiments. They may or may not result in claims. Consequently, *the human being (as "experimenter") is always part of each of "his risks"* either retained or insured. He is unable to detach himself completely from "his risks." The human being represents quite a substantial part of many risks dealt with in the insurance industry.

Examples of Risks at the Limits of Insurability

We have frequently underlined the significance of subjective aspects when determining the insurability of risks. It is therefore obvious that when specific risks are examined as to their insurability, subjective aspects may arise which do not always conincide with the opinions of the reader. In the following examples we shall proceed according to the following principles:

1. The risks should be checked using the nine insurability criteria discussed in this study.
2. It is usually easy to recognize that the question "insurable or not" depends on only few criteria. We therefore want to concentrate on the *decisive*

criteria in each case and emphazise them in the examples.

3. We shall keep our arguments as objective as possible and hope thereby to find extensive agreement with the reader. We shall therefore deal with risks which lie at the limits of insurability for the entire community of professional risk carriers or, for reasons of principle, for *each* individual risk carrier. In other words, we have to do with risks located near the objective limit of uninsurability.

Risks which a given risk carrier cannot bear for capacity, utility, or other reasons of an individual nature but which other risk carriers are willing to bear will be excluded from the examples, since their insurability is based largely on subjective aspects, already dealt with in detail in Chapter 4. Suggestions of how to overcome subjective difficulties and to extend the subjective area of insurability were given in that chapter in the form of principles and recommendations.

Example 1: Natural Catastrophes (earthquake, storm, flood)

To cover natural catastrophes is one of the tasks of the insurance industry. It should try to grant such covers wherever required. In order to achieve this, certain guidelines are recommended:

1. As mentioned in Section 4.1.3, a tight accumulation control is extremely important in the case of catastrophe risks.
2. According to Section 4.4.2, as much information as possible should be obtained about the catastrophe risks to be insured.
3. Close cooperation between all the risk carriers participating in the cover of a natural catastrophe risk is important to achieve an optimal exchange of information and optimal utilization of capacity.

4. Natural catastrophes should be rated separately from other lines of business. This helps to make premiums commensurate with the risk (i.e., self-supporting). There exists less of a temptation to underrate. Separate rating also facilitates the accumulation control between the various lines of business.
5. Appropriate reserves must be set aside and built up by means of adequate premiums.
6. A price must be asked for the capacity made available. This price should increase more than proportionately with the capacity (see Principle 15).
7. Preventive protection measures for objects in areas exposed to natural catastrophe hazards should be encouraged by means of premium reductions.

In natural catastrophe areas containing an accumulation of objects of value, the worldwide capacity of private risk carriers might not be sufficient to cover the maximum possible loss. The *critical insurability criterion* in such a context will therefore often be *the maximum possible loss.* If cover limits were set too stingily by the private insurance carriers, it would not be worthwhile for the individual to seek cover for his risks with them. Persistent seekers of cover would look around for another risk carrier, and the state might feel compelled to assume this role.

The state might also be called in as risk carrier if the private risk carriers were not able to meet their liabilities as a result of a "super-catastrophe." In view of such possibilities, is it not better for the private insurance industry on its own initiative to try to win over the state as risk carrier in advance? The state could, for example, provide excess of loss facilities in the super-catastrophe area.

In the case of natural catastrophes, as with all risks for which it is difficult to satisfy criteria c and d (high average loss amount and large average period of time between two loss occurrences), we unfortunately observe again and again how the insurance industry cuts the ground from under its own feet through unsound competition. The more time that has elapsed since the last large loss, the further the premiums sink below the justified minimum level. Such a development is regrettable and has already proved costly for many a risk carrier; it contradicts completely the prerequisites outlined previously by means of which natural catastrophes should be made insurable.

Example 2: Business Interruption (LOP = loss of profit) Cover Against Strikes

In general, we consider it to be *contrary to public policy* to cover an employer against strikes. Such a cover furnishes the employer with a weapon which can be abused, and the risk carrier indirectly affects the relations between labor and management, which is not his job. In addition to public policy, the *insurance premium* is also a critical criterion here; a proper premium could hardly be calculated and therefore a huge security loading would have to be charged.

However, a fire LOP cover which does not exclude strikes lies within the insurability area, since burning down a factory is not a usual way of solving a labor conflict. The fire LOP cover is therefore a proper object for insurance and not contrary to public policy.

Example 3: Nationalization Risks

In accordance with the remark in Section 4.6.5 and Principle 18, we consider neither moral hazard nor public policy to be a critical criterion. In countries with a risk of nationalization the criteria of *degree of randomness* (is nationalization already likely?) and *insurance premium* (incalculability) are critical, as well as *legal restrictions* (cover can contradict intentions of the government). In case of insurance of a nationalization risk, a clause should ensure that the insured not be fully compensated twice for expropriation (by the state, as well as by the insurer).

Example 4: Trivial Risks

According to Section 4.6.2 and Principle 22, trivial risks are in general *not suitable for insurance (contrary to public policy).* However, such risks are repeatedly covered because of carelessness, lack of knowledge, inconsistency, competitiveness, and other reasons.

Example 5: Kidnapping Cover

Such covers discussed in Section 4.6.5 should not be branded as a matter of course as uninsurable. We pointed out that covers which could be used to encourage crime should be avoided. The critical criterion in the case of covers against ransom demands in conjunction with kidnapping is not public policy but *cover limits* and in some countries *legal restrictions.* In addition to deductibles, limits of cover and proportional participation of the insured in the risk we mentioned a silence clause which obliges kidnapped parties to conceal, even deny, the existence of a ransom insurance. Further problematical questions are the *insurance premium* and the *moral hazard* (staging a kidnapping).

Example 6:

All "covers" aimed at evading taxes or tax fraud or violation of laws or legal stipulations are *contrary to public policy, do not fulfil the criterion of randomness,* and infringe upon *legal restrictions.* They should not be granted.

Example 7: Cover Against Civil Commotion

In our opinion, such a cover is generally not insurable, because the premium for it cannot be calculated. Here the *insurance premium* is the decisive criterion. The protection of the individual, physically as well as materially, against civil commotion is in the first place a duty of the state.

Example 8: Insurance Cover for Overseas Investments (political risks)

Investment risk insurance should be granted, if at all, by the state and not by the private insurance industry; in contrast to the nationalization risks in Example 3, the applicants for cover are here not inhabitants of the state which is the cause of the nationalization risk but of another state. Investment risk guarantees are also often a form of economic aid and not based on commercial considerations. The private risk carrier must, however, set up his underwriting policy on a commercial basis. The decisive criteria for the rejection of investment risk guarantees are the *degree of randomness* and the *insurance premium*.

Example 9: Motor Liability Excess of Loss Reinsurance Cover

In accordance with Section 4.8, we consider such a cover in principle to be justifiable only when the index clause is incorporated into the treaty to *limit the cover*. This requirement is all the more urgent the higher the priority and the greater the covered layer.

Example 10: Cover of Punitive Damages

Principle: Punitive damages should not be passed on to others. If such covers cannot be blocked by means of *legal restrictions,* they should be rejected because of *moral hazard*, but even more importantly because of *public policy* considerations.

1. Fines should not be insurable. Such an insurance cover would in any case very likely be rejected by the supervisory authorities.

2. Some time ago the Insurance Services Office was pressing, however, without success, for the exclusion of punitive damages from insurance policies in the United States.*

*The following two examples represent rather extreme verdicts in courts of first instance involving punitive damages:

1. National Service Industries Ltd. was commissioned to remove the furniture from an apartment owned by a real estate firm, Investors Funding Corp. in El Dorado Towers in Montgomery County, Maryland. An employee of National Service Industries raped and stabbed to death the occupant of a neighboring apartment and was sentenced to life imprisonment; this employee had, unknown to National Service, formerly been convicted of armed robbery and was on parole. The court awarded the spouse of the victim and his two sons compensatory damages of $2,355,000 to be paid in equal proportions by Investors Funding and National Services with an additional $11 million in punitive damages to be paid solely by Investors Funding! The employees of El Dorado Towers had been in contact with the movers on the day in question and had not expelled them from the building, although the employees of the moving firm were drunk. The responsibility for this was laid by the court on Investors Funding, then held to be liable for these enormous punitive damages.

2. The Ford Pinto case: The Ford Motor Company has been ordered to pay a total of $128.5 million to the injured survivor of a serious automobile accident and the dependents of the woman driver killed in the accident. This enormous amount was determined by a court in Santa Ana (California), which charged Ford with not having undertaken any remedial action on its small Pinto model, although it knew that there was danger of explosion in the gasoline tank. Endangering the safety of consumers "knowingly" or "intentionally" can lead to very severe penalties under American law. Ford has appealed the decision as "unreasonable and unjust" and maintains that the Pinto fulfills all government safety requirements.

The accident occurred in 1972 on a California highway. As the result of difficulties with the Pinto's motor another vehicle collided with it from behind and the gasoline tank of the Pinto, located in the rear, exploded. The woman driver perished in the flames and a 13-year-old boy suffered third-degree burns. Ford has been ordered to pay the woman's survivors about $650,000, whereas the injured passenger is to receive $2.8 million in compensatory damages and *$125 million in punitive damages*. This is the largest amount ever awarded by a court in respect of an automobile accident.

Example 11: Awards for Mental Suffering and the Like

We mentioned earlier the insurance principle that compensation paid to an injured party in a liability case should not be higher than the actual loss incurred. The underlying injury can be of a physical and/or a nonphysical nature. To uphold the idea of insurance in the case of nonphysical injury is difficult since the extent of the nonphysical damage suffered by the insured is often defined by individuals outside the insurance business (judges). Court practice in recent years in various countries has tended more and more to award the injured party substantial sums for nonphysical reasons (e.g., in the form of awards for pain and suffering). Although this practice is understandable and may emanate from humanitarian considerations, it contradicts the above-mentioned principle of insurance and thus pushes whole groups of risks into the area of uninsurability. Here the *maximum possible loss,* the *insurance premium,* and *public policy* become critical criteria.

As already indicated in Section 4.6.3, medical malpractice insurance in the United States has practically been pushed to the limits of insurability.

Example 12: Speculative Entrepreneurial Risks

In general, we consider speculative entrepreneurial risks to be uninsurable because they are *contrary to public policy* (see Section 4.6.1 and Principle 21).

Example 13: Entrepreneurial Risks

In products liability, defects in products delivered to customers often cannot be insured, but the *consequences* of such defects can. This practice can in general be regarded as justified. Although the consequences of defective products are less easy to survey and more difficult to evaluate than the actual defects themselves, they are also less *subject to moral hazard,* and the insurer does not have to largely identify himself with the entrepreneur, which is not his job (*public policy*). In the language of this study, this can be expressed as follows:

With an insurance covering the defects of products sold in the market, the criterion *insurance premium* is usually better satisfied than with a cover of consequential loss arising from such defects. In respect of the criteria *moral hazard* and *public policy*, the reverse is the case. In the geometric model this means that in the first case the projection on the insurance premium axis is usually closer to zero; in the second case the projections on the moral hazard and public policy axes are closer. The advantages in the second case are usually greater than the advantage in the first case, which is why cover of the consequences of product defects is more likely to be considered insurable than cover of product defects themselves.

Concluding Remark

At the end of Chapter 2 we mentioned that the nine insurability criteria relate to the realms of actuarial science, experience, business ethics, law, and commerce. This study has therefore dealt with interdisciplinary fields and touched upon a broad spectrum of topics.

It would hardly be possible to list all the literature treating these various topics in a bibliography. Since, in addition, no external literary sources were used in compiling this work, we have also refrained from introducing references into the text.